FOOD & DRINK

COOKBOOK

D0716270

THE
FOOD & DRINK
COOKBOOK

Michael Barry, Jill Goolden, Chris Kelly

BRITISH BROADCASTING CORPORATION

The authors would like to acknowledge with gratitude the help
and advice given by Eleri Evans.

Published by the British Broadcasting Corporation,
35 Marylebone High Street, London W1M 4AA

First published 1985

ISBN 0 563 20426 5

Set in 10/11 pt Rockwell Light and printed by
The Bath Press, Avon

CONTENTS

Introduction	7
Pizza and Pasta	9
Chianti	18
Continental Cuts	19
Non-alcoholic Drinks	24
Quick 'Cook-in' Sauces	25
White Wines of Character	32
Mushrooms	33
Sherry	39
Vegetables	41
The Bottle v. the Tap: Mineral Water	50
Rice	53
Lager	60
Apples	61
Liquid Gold: Cider and Apple Juice	68
Christmas Cooking	71
Celebration Fizz	81
Meals for One	83
The Food and Drink £10 Challenge	89

INTRODUCTION

For me, there will always be two abiding memories of television in the fifties – the First Age of Television, as it's now rather grandly called. One is of a couple of loose-limbed figures, apparently swimming in grey soup on the tiny screen – Bill and Ben the Flowerpot Men, with guest appearances by Weed, who, judging by his voice, must have been one of the few castrati to achieve stardom at the BBC. And the other vision that period conjures up is of television cooks. There they stood, some with beards and some without, leaning on a table and telling us how simple soufflés really are. On that score, I don't believe them to this day. There have been several generations of excellent television cooks since then, who have brought new ideas to the presentation of cooking on television, and introduced a wealth of fresh thinking about food, but basically most programmes still depend on a single presenter demonstrating recipes. We wanted the *Food and Drink* programme to do something a bit different, to take a fresh approach to the subject. Instead of focusing purely on cooking, we set out to embrace every aspect of the theme.

What makes it different? To begin with, *Food and Drink* is a weekly magazine that reports on topical issues. Not surprisingly, these frequently reflect our increasing national concern with healthy eating. Food is one of the great social and political footballs of the 1980s. Whether we're talking about proposed legislation for detailing fat content on labels, or diets that are believed to discourage delinquency, or the effects of the EEC on the independent British cheese producer, food is news at every level. We aim not just to listen in on the great debate, but to lead it. We believe our role should include watching over the food manufacturing industry, monitoring its methods, testing its claims, and bringing news of its innovations – and we do it, we hope, in an entertaining and informative way.

Two more essential elements in the *Food and Drink* mix, though, are the contributions of our resident experts. Michael Barry, the Crafty Cook, has developed a sleeves-up style in the kitchen which slices right through any snobbery that might still cling to cuisine. His suggestions are original, simple and delicious. Jill Goolden, our drinks expert, has rejected the snooty view of many wine writers who treat the subject as the exclusive province of the *cognoscenti*, and deals with wine as the commodity that is available to all of us in supermarkets.

Significantly, in any case, the programme isn't called *Food and Wine*, and with the help of specialist guests, Jill offers wily tips on drinks as diverse as mineral water, canned lager and non-alcoholic vermouth.

The idea behind this book is to reflect some aspects of the series. We know people like our recipes because we get a tremendous response from viewers. After one programme featured Anton Mosimann, *Maître Chef des Cuisines* at London's Dorchester Hotel, preparing a meal for a Sheffield family of seven for less than a tenner (the details are included here!), we received 60,000 requests for our fact sheet – that is from one in every twenty-five families watching. In line with the general approach of the programmes, Michael Barry's recipes have been grouped into separate topics or themes – mushrooms, continental cuts of meat, quick-cook sauces, apples, Christmas cooking and so on. His recipes are brief and easy to follow – and cut through many of the myths that are perpetuated about special methods of preparation, such as tricky sauces or whatever. They work, too, as I should know – as presenter of the programmes I've often had the chance of sampling them in the studio kitchen! Where appropriate, information is given about the availability of ingredients, and what to look for when choosing them, or about fat content or other points of interest. And the recipes reflect a wide spread of national cuisines, from China to India, Greece, Italy, the Caribbean, to traditional English country cooking. Jill Goolden has contributed to each chapter a feature on wines and other drinks, alcoholic and non-alcoholic, including cider, mineral waters and sparkling wines.

One speciality of *Food and Drink* is its guest features, and the book takes this into account. As well as Anton Mosimann's £10 feast, you'll find here Jane Grigson's Meal for One. All in all, a tempting and varied mix, and we hope you enjoy it.

Chris Kelly

PIZZA AND PASTA
Chianti

PIZZA AND PASTA

Pizza and pasta – the two most famous Italian foods – are certainly the two most abused (ice-cream comes a close third, but that's another story). Pizzas are now a commonplace food in Britain, and pasta (at least in its canteen form of spaghetti bolognese) is being eaten by a third generation of *habitués*.

PIZZA

Few of our towns are now without a pizza parlour competing with Chinese and Indian takeaways. And the varieties to be found in supermarkets – fresh or more usually frozen – make the mind boggle. Hawaiian pizzas complete with pineapple cubes have arrived! But such outrageous travesties have not escaped the notice of the Italians. In Naples, the home of the pizza, a society for the protection of the genuine article has been formed. It insists on pure ingredients, classic toppings and swift cooking in the traditional beehive-shaped brick oven fired by beechwood. So to test whether the Italians were being over-sensitive, or whether the British were being undernourished, we asked six expatriate Neapolitans to test a range of British shop-bought pizzas. Their reactions were unanimous: all the pizzas were bad, most were dreadful, and the bigger the supermarket the worse the pizza. The thick doughy bases and skimpy, unauthentic ingredients outraged them. Strangely enough, the only shop-bought pizza they could stomach was the French bread version; they thought the base crispy and light and the toppings generous. But they all agreed that anyone could do better at home, even without a beehive-oven and a beechwood fire.

Quick Pizza Dough
(Makes three individual pizzas)

Vitamin C is the crafty quick ingredient here. It's available in powdered form in any chemist. Don't be tempted to use any more than we suggest or to substitute dried yeast. Try spreading the dough with your hands rather than a rolling pin, it's easier and more authentic.

Traditionally, pizza dough takes twelve hours to rise. This version (Neapolitan-approved) takes just fifteen minutes and produces pizzas that are crisp, savoury and subtle. Do heat the oven properly and try preheating the baking sheet or a ceramic tile before putting the pizza on top.

---

1 oz (25 gms) fresh yeast
$\frac{1}{4}$ tsp ascorbic acid (vitamin C powder)
1 lb (450 gms) white flour
$\frac{1}{2}$ tsp salt
$\frac{1}{2}$ pint (300 ml) hot water
1 tbsp olive oil

Mix the yeast and vitamin C in a little of the water. Add to the flour, then mix with all the other ingredients and the rest of the water in a warmed bowl. Knead until smooth. Leave in a warm place to rise for 15 minutes. Knead again, then divide the dough into three balls and spread each ball into an 8-inch (20-cm) pizza base. Add one of the fillings below and bake at gas mark 9, 475°F (240°C) for 15 minutes, putting the pizzas on a preheated ceramic or metal base in the oven. Eat them hot!

We are giving suggestions for four traditional fillings but, notwithstanding the sensibilities of the Neapolitans, you can of course experiment with your own. The first suggestion, *Margheurita*, is the most loved filling in Naples, where its more fanciful inhabitants claim that it was inspired by the colours of the Italian national flag: the green of the basil, the white of the Mozzarella and the red of the tomatoes. By the way, in all these recipes fresh herbs are wonderful if you can get them (many delicatessens and supermarkets now stock them). If not, dried herbs are fine and often used by the Italians themselves. If you are using fresh herbs, double the quantities given in the following recipes.

Margheurita
(For each pizza)

2 tbsp chopped tinned Italian tomatoes
2 tbsp thinly sliced Mozzarella cheese
1 tsp Parmesan cheese
1 tsp dried basil leaves
1 tsp dried oregano
Salt and pepper
1 tsp olive oil

Spread the tomatoes over the dough, leaving $\frac{1}{2}$ inch (1 cm) around the edge. Sprinkle the Mozzarella over the tomatoes, then add the Parmesan, herbs and seasoning. Lastly pour on the olive oil. Bake.

Mushroom
(For each pizza)

2 tbsp thinly sliced Mozzarella cheese
2 oz (50 gms) thinly sliced mushrooms
1 chopped clove garlic
Salt and pepper
1 tsp oregano
2 tbsp olive oil

Spread the cheese and mushrooms over the dough, leaving $\frac{1}{2}$ inch (1 cm) around the edge. Then sprinkle the garlic, seasoning and oregano over the base, followed by the olive oil. Bake.

Marinara
(For each pizza)

2 tbsp chopped Italian tomatoes
4 anchovy fillets
6 black olives
1 tsp capers
Salt and pepper
1 tbsp olive oil or anchovy oil

Spread the tomatoes over the dough, leaving $\frac{1}{2}$ inch (1 cm) around the edge. Split the anchovy fillets and arrange them like the spokes of a wheel. Then lay the olives and capers on top. Season lightly. Pour over the oil (using the oil from the anchovy tin is a good idea). Bake.

Double Mozzarella
(For each pizza)

4 oz (100 gms) Mozzarella cheese, half sliced, half coarsely grated
Salt and pepper
1 tsp basil
1 tsp oregano
1 tbsp Parmesan cheese
2 tbsp olive oil

Put the sliced Mozzarella cheese in a layer over the dough, season, and then sprinkle with the herbs. Add the grated Mozzarella and Parmesan and sprinkle the oil over. Bake.

PASTA

If you think the Neapolitans take their pizza seriously, then consider the excesses to which Italy's premier pasta company has gone. The directors of *Voiello* have hired one of the world's top industrial designers (an Italian, of course) to create an entirely new shape for them. Sig. Giuggiaro, previously renowned for designing Fiats rather than food, has produced the first-ever 'designer' pasta. He's called it *Marille*. Thousands of man-hours spent at his drawing board have produced a quite extraordinary object. I can best describe it as two parallel tubes with a wing on one side. *Marille* has become something of a status symbol in Italy's dining rooms, and it is now in such short supply that packets are exchanged *under* the counter for exorbitant sums.

But while we might laugh at such gastronomic extremes, the basic design of *Marille* makes sense. It has small grooves inside its tubes which retain plenty of sauce on the journey from plate to mouth.

There are many different shapes and textures to be found among pastas and each is carefully designed to accompany different types of sauces. British tinned-food manufacturers – true to form – have taken this one stage further and produced bizarre varieties such as space invaders-shaped pasta aimed at children's imagination and their mothers' purses. They may look different but they all seem to taste curiously alike. Our advice is to stick to the traditional pastas. The sauces which best complement them are as follows.

Spirals are good for creamy sauces which stick in the complex folds and curlicues. *Tagliatelle* (flat noodles which are white, yellow or green depending on whether they are plain, egg- or spinach-flavoured) is often eaten with rich sauces for which it makes an excellent base. Cheese, especially Parmesan, is often added for its flavour and slightly granular texture. *Conghile*, or snail shells, are little pasta pockets which are good for holding sauces with chunky ingredients. In Italy, spaghetti is often eaten with very simple flavourings, such as olive oil, garlic and Parmesan cheese, or just with butter and cheese. The recipes below are for dried pasta which you can buy in packets from any grocer's or supermarket. Fresh pasta is beginning to be more available and you could try it. It cooks much more quickly – about three minutes in boiling water – but remember it is more expensive and doesn't keep that long.

Here are some suggestions, beginning with a sauce for *Marille*, in the unlikely event of your acquiring some. If not, it's great with spaghetti.

Ragù alla Bolognese
(Serves four)

This is the authentic bolognese sauce. It is very rich and creamy, and makes enough to accompany $\frac{3}{4}$ lb (350 gms) uncooked pasta.

---

8 oz (225 gms) lean minced beef
4 tbsp olive oil
8 oz (225 gms) finely chopped onion
1 chopped clove garlic
2 oz (50 gms) chopped chicken livers
2 oz (50 gms) grated carrot
15-oz tin Italian tomatoes
2 tbsp tomato purée
Salt and pepper
1 tsp dried basil
1 tsp dried oregano
$\frac{1}{2}$ tsp thyme

Sauté the beef in the oil until brown. Add the onion, garlic, chicken livers and carrot and sauté for 1 minute more before adding the tomatoes and tomato purée. Then season the mixture and simmer for 45 minutes, adding a little water when necessary to keep the sauce moist. Add the herbs 5 minutes before serving.

Carbonara
(Serves four)

This rich but simple recipe is good with pasta spirals as they have a sufficiently large surface area to 'cook' the eggs. The crisp, fried salami and cheese add an interesting contrast of textures. This recipe makes enough to accompany $\frac{3}{4}$ lb (350 gms) uncooked pasta.

2 oz (50 gms) finely sliced salami
1 tbsp olive oil
3 eggs
2 fl oz (50 ml) double cream
2 oz (50 gms) Parmesan cheese
Salt and pepper

Cut the salami into matchsticks and fry in a little oil until crisp. Beat the eggs with the cream. Cook the pasta spirals until just tender. Drain and return the pasta to the pan. Add the egg and cream mixture and stir off the heat until the eggs have scrambled. Mix in the salami and Parmesan and season generously. Serve piping hot.

Gorgonzola alla Creme
(Serves four)

This is again a rich but simple sauce – perfect for the flat green noodles called *tagliatelle verdi* which get their colouring from the spinach they are made with. The sauce is a speciality of Sicily and the quantities given make enough to accompany $\frac{3}{4}$ lb (350 gms) uncooked pasta.

4 oz (100 gms) Gorgonzola cheese
3 oz (75 gms) butter
2 fl oz (50 ml) double cream
Black pepper

Cream the cheese and butter together (a processor or blender does this very well). Shape into a roll and chill. Cook the pasta. Slice the roll into $\frac{1}{2}$-inch (1-cm) sections and melt them gently in the cream. When the sauce is smooth, but not boiling, toss the noodles in it. Serve with plenty of black pepper.

Zucchini and Snails
(Serves four)

Not an Italian takeover of a French leftover, but a pasta called *conghile* that's made to look like snail shells. This is a vegetarian sauce that's great for summer eating. In small quantities it makes a good starter. The amounts given make enough sauce to accompany $\frac{3}{4}$ lb (350 gms) uncooked pasta.

1 lb (450 gms) courgettes (zucchini in Italian)
2 fl oz (50 ml) olive oil
1 finely chopped onion
1 chopped clove garlic
1 tsp oregano
$\frac{1}{2}$ tsp basil
4 tbsp tomato purée
$\frac{1}{2}$ cup water
Grated Parmesan cheese (to serve)

Cook the *conghile* according to the instructions on the packet. Wash and trim the courgettes. Slice them into $\frac{1}{4}$-inch ($\frac{1}{2}$-cm) rounds then fry briskly in the oil for 2 minutes, with the onion. Add all the other ingredients and stir until well-mixed. Simmer for 3 minutes and pour over the cooked shells. Serve with Parmesan cheese – freshly grated if possible.

CHIANTI

Chianti is the traditional partner for pasta, the inevitable companion for a plate of spaghetti bolognese. And since pizza and pasta are now found all over the world, not surprisingly Chianti has become a shade over-exposed and over-produced as a result. Not to put too fine a point on it, much Chianti sold today is far from good. At its best, this light, soft, generally youthful red wine, made from both red and white grapes in the Tuscany area surrounding Florence, is the perfect match for filling, often spicy, pasta dishes. But before buying your next bottle, it's worth finding out a little about Chianti.

The attractive straw-covered flasks, so dearly loved by Italian restaurants, are definitely to be avoided. They may be attractive but these outmoded *fiascos* or flasks usually conceal second-rate wine at an inflated price. When glass bottles were first blown they were spherical and so baskets with flat bases were used to keep the bottle upright. Glass-blowing techniques have come a long way since then, and the flasks are now redundant frills, used simply to attract unwitting customers to buy mediocre wine.

The best Chianti comes in straight-sided Bordeaux-style bottles. All Chianti legally has the right to claim the Italian quality status of DOC (*Denominazione di Origine Controllata*), so finding that on the label is no particular guarantee. The better wines generally come from the traditional heart of the region and so earn themselves the right to call themselves Chianti Classico. Most of these wines also show a black cockerel somewhere on the label. This is the emblem of an exclusive club whose members are all well-respected genuine Chianti producers.

CONTINENTAL CUTS
Non-alcoholic Drinks

CONTINENTAL CUTS

1985 has seen a milestone in our eating habits. For the first time since we've kept such records, our consumption of red meat (beef, lamb and pork) has fallen below our consumption of poultry. The national dish is no longer roast beef but grilled chicken. There are several reasons for this change, the chief one being the wide availability of low-priced, battery-reared poultry. But there's another reason which is not connected with the housekeeping. Red meat's been getting a bad press: it's high in saturated fat and therefore bad for your heart, goes the argument. Health campaigners now point to the post-war trend in agriculture where intensively-reared animals have produced meat higher in saturated fats. And while a newly health-conscious nation has responded by buying less, our butchers are poorly equipped to help. British butchery, now largely destroyed as a craft by electric saws and frozen meat, was never very subtle even at its best. We cut our meat at the bone junctions into big 'joints', very often wrapping them in extra fat if the cuts are dry or need dressing up.

Continental butchery on the other hand cuts meat up into muscle groups. This has several advantages. It cooks better with less shrinkage and distortion. The joints, often boneless, are very carefully and attractively presented. And, most important of all, the lean meat contains less fatty muscle and excess outer fat is trimmed off rather than added on. It's a more expensive way to buy meat but is not always more costly in the end as there's far less waste. The English and European styles of butchery are different for all the cuts, whether it's a joint for roasting or chunks for a stew. And although fat contributes greatly to the flavour of meat, there is quite enough left in continental cuts for that purpose. If they were available here they might give red meat a new lease of life.

Fortunately, this style of butchery has now crossed the Channel. Not only Harrods, but also a number of good butchers and supermarkets, are now offering continental cuts. Sainsbury's, Safeway's and Tesco's are the leaders among the latter. So the new cuts are now relatively easy to obtain. How easy are they to cook? These recipes are for some of the more recognisable cuts: noisettes of lamb, the heart of a lamb chop without fat or bone; butterfly lamb cutlets, split to resemble a giant butterfly; lamb kebab, chunks of lean leg of lamb;

and goulash (also known as bourguignon), lean beef cut into generous cubes without tendon or gristle.

The recipes are all attractive enough for special occasions and, appropriately enough, use very little fat themselves.

Lamb Noisettes with Garlic Sauce
(Serves four)

This is a delicate and delicious dish with a hint, rather than a hammer blow, of garlic. If you can't obtain noisettes, cut your own using the eye of thick lamb chops and then split them in half across the grain. To improve the 'healthiness' of the dish, try using an oil low in saturated fats such as sunflower, soya or olive oil.

---

1 King Edward potato
4 cloves garlic, peeled and crushed, with the green centre removed
$\frac{1}{2}$ pint (300 ml) milk (skimmed if preferred)
8 thick lamb noisettes, or chops
2 tsp oil for frying
Salt and pepper

Peel and dice the potato and place in a saucepan with the garlic cloves. Add the milk and cook gently for about 15 minutes, or until the potato is soft. Blend, process or sieve the sauce to make a smooth purée.

Meanwhile, heat the oil in a heavy frying pan until very hot. Fry the noisettes for about 2 minutes on each side, depending on how well-cooked you like your meat. Season when cooked. Pour the sauce on to a serving dish and place the noisettes on top.

This dish is particularly good served with green beans or a tossed green salad.

Butterfly Chops (Côtelettes Premières) with Mustard and Redcurrant Jelly
(Serves four)

Butterfly chops are cut to open out into a double chop shape, but this variant of a favourite combination can be made with English cuts as well. A little extra redcurrant jelly and mustard served with it always goes down well, as do new potatoes and some steamed broccoli.

2 tbsp redcurrant jelly
1 tbsp French mustard
4 butterfly chops
Salt and pepper

Heat the grill until very hot. Mix together the redcurrant jelly and mustard. Baste the chops with this, season and place under the grill. Baste frequently until the chops are cooked as you like them: 3 minutes each side for rare, 4 minutes for medium and 5 for well-done. Season and serve.

Hungarian Goulash
(Serves six)

This dish is one of the most easy and heartening casseroles I know. A complete meal in itself, it calls for soup bowls, chunks of wholemeal brown bread and hearty appetites.

2 lbs (900 gms) cubes of lean beef
1 tbsp oil
2 peeled and sliced onions
4 tbsp tomato purée
1 tbsp paprika
1½ lbs (700 gms) potatoes
1 tsp caraway seeds
Salt and pepper

Brown the meat in the oil in a heavy casserole or pan. Then add the onions and cook until translucent, stirring from time to time. Add the tomato purée, paprika and enough water to cover it all. Simmer for 45 minutes. Cut the peeled potatoes into walnut-sized chunks and add to the pan, together with the caraway seeds. Season well, and simmer for a further 20 minutes. If the sauce is too thin, thicken it with 1 teaspoon of cornflour mixed with a little water – or mash one or two of the potatoes well and return to the sauce. Noodles are best with this, and a little sour cream.

Lamb and Fruit Kebabs
1 kebab per person

We tend to associate kebabs with Greece – clear light, wine-dark seas and a bouzouki under your window at two in the morning. But in fact kebabs are made all round the world and this recipe comes from the French colonies in the South Pacific. Exotic and delicious, it's best served with rice – saffron pilau makes it really special.

For each kebab:

6 oz (175 gms) lamb, cubed
Juice and rind of 1 lemon
Pinch of cinnamon or allspice
$\frac{1}{4}$ green pepper
4 pineapple cubes (fresh or tinned)
4 apricot halves or peach quarters (fresh or tinned)
Juice and rind of 1 orange
Salt and pepper

Marinade the lamb in the lemon juice and cinnamon for 2 hours. Deseed the green pepper, remove the pith and cut into 1-inch ($2\frac{1}{2}$-cm) squares. Using either metal or wood skewers, prepare each kebab by threading on in turn a chunk of pepper, then lamb, then pineapple, then apricot, and so on, finishing with a piece of pepper. Grill the kebabs for 3 minutes, then turn and grill for 4–5 minutes longer. Meanwhile, bring the grated rind of lemon and orange to the boil in the orange juice and simmer for 2 minutes. Add the marinade and all the other juices and season well. Serve separately with the kebabs.

NON-ALCOHOLIC DRINKS

Health- and weight-conscious drinkers may want to cut down on alcohol, without necessarily giving up drink. Now they can, by choosing from a range of new non-alcoholic drinks simply light years away from lemonade. Not only are the subtle flavours of established drinks successfully being copied, but a range of new concoctions is being dreamed up – novelties and breakthroughs in their own right.

Aperitifs such as Campari, Vermouth, Pernod and even Scotch and American Ginger or Rum and Coke are now available in harmless, and convincing, alcohol-free taste-alikes. You can even find de-alcoholised still and sparkling wines and beers. But not all are equally good; there are some over-sugared frauds among the predominantly dry, bitter, sharp new school.

A chasm of difference exists between grape juice and de-alcoholised wine. During the process of fermentation, yeast consumes all, or nearly all, of the sugar present in the grape juice, or must, and turns it into alcohol. This makes a much drier drink than the original grape juice, while still retaining the flavour of the fruit. The alcohol is then removed by a scientific process, but the drink, of course, remains dry.

Louis Pasteur may well have believed he had a breakthrough on his hands when he cracked the secrets of fermentation way back in 1859. But more than a century later in the all-slimming, all-skipping 1980s, it is the chap who worked out how to de-alcoholise wine and make, at last, grown-up soft drinks who now deserves the praise.

The most likeable de-alcoholised wines, suffering the least after-effects of the de-alcoholisation process, are Jung's Weisslack: flowery, medium-dry German 'wine'; and the sparkling Schloss Boosenberg, which makes a good base for Bucks Fizz (mixed with an equal quantity of orange juice). Pastis seems to be one of the easiest hard liquors to mimic and the anise taste-alikes are quite delicious. Two good brands are Blancart and Katell Roc.

Katell Roc have invented two successful and imaginative new drinks: Americano, a dark-red, bitter-sweet vermouth type; and the tart and sophisticated Aperitivo. Another recommendable bitter drink is the Campari substitute, Kas Bitter de Luxe.

De-alcoholised beer can be rather watery and unexciting. Brands with more flavour than most are Clausthaler and Panther.

All non-alcoholic drinks are best served well-chilled.

QUICK 'COOK-IN' SAUCES
White Wines of Character

QUICK 'COOK-IN' SAUCES

In 1984 Britons spent nearly £50 million on sauces – no, not tomato, HP or brown sauces but a new category in sauces that's booming in popularity: cook-in sauces. They come in packets, tins, sachets and cartons: Sweet and Sour, Curry, Chilli Con Carne, Mexican, French, Italian and Chinese. In fact, every kind of sauce you can imagine and some you probably can't. Why do we buy them? Well, convenience must be one answer, and economy another – it's an opportunity to taste exotic flavours without having to buy lots of pricy ingredients. Either way, cook-in sauces are big business in our shops and go down in a big way at our dinner tables. So do they deliver their promise of convenience and economy along with an acceptable taste? We examined everything about them from how readable their instructions were to how well they flavoured their respective dishes, but to simplify the test we confined our attention to Chilli Con Carne, Curry and Sweet and Sour sauces.

Few of the sauces were really impressive, particularly on the taste tests. Packet sauces were almost always better (and cheaper) than canned sauces. It didn't surprise us that the sauces with the fewest additives and the most natural ingredients were always the winners. So the results were almost always predictable from the list of contents alone. Sharwoods, which makes a variety of exotic sauces, came out as the best of a pretty average bunch.

We then turned our attention to how convenient it can be to make your own quick-cook sauces. They've been keeping my family and friends fed for years, and their origins are truly cosmopolitan. They may emanate from the Peloponnese to Peking but they all have one thing in common: none takes more than five minutes to make from start to finish. (And they have no additives or emulsifiers in them.)

Steak in Mustard Cream

This recipe is especially good with steaks, but also works a treat with other meats and other flavours: chicken breasts with chopped chives instead of mustard, or veal escalopes with juniper berries are two examples. It's certainly a rich sauce but you can serve it from time to time without too many pangs of conscience. Don't let on how easy or quick it is, please! I've been getting away with it for years.

For each person:

Salt and pepper
1 steak (entrecôte or sirloin)
1 tbsp butter
1 dsp oil
2 tbsp double cream
1 tsp grain mustard

Season the steak. Heat the butter and oil until they foam. Add the steak and fry on one side for 2 minutes. Turn it over, add the cream and stir in the mustard. Cook for 1 minute more and serve.

Courgette and Tomato Provençale
(Serves four)

This reflects my liking for hot but crisp vegetables. The technique of stir-shaking works well for all vegetables that you can eat and enjoy raw. Courgettes are one, try them sliced thinly in salad.

2 tbsp olive oil
1 lb (450 gms) medium-sliced courgettes
2 tbsp tomato purée
1 tsp garlic salt
$\frac{1}{2}$ tsp oregano
$\frac{1}{2}$ tsp basil

Heat the oil until very hot. Throw in the courgettes, cover the pan and shake. Add the tomato purée, garlic salt, oregano and basil. Shake again. Cook for 1 minute and serve.

Sweet and Sour Prawns
(Serves two)

We tend to think of sweet and sour sauce as a kind of red and glutinous Chinese tomato ketchup. And to add insult to injury, much of the sweet and sour sauce served in Chinese takeaway restaurants is heavily dosed with monosodium glutamate. Made properly in China, the sauce's colour varies from region to region; and at its best is subtle and spicy. This version comes from the northern part of China and is brown, not red, to set off the prawns. Serve it with rice and stir-fried bean sprouts.

1 tbsp cornflour
4 tbsp orange juice
4 tbsp soya sauce
1 tbsp brown sugar
1 tbsp cider vinegar
$\frac{1}{2}$ tsp garlic salt
$\frac{1}{2}$ tsp ground ginger
1 dsp oil
1 tbsp tomato purée (optional)
2 tbsp crushed pineapple (optional)
8 oz (225 gms) peeled prawns

Mix the cornflour with the orange juice until smooth. Mix with all the other ingredients except the prawns and bring to the boil in a saucepan, stirring regularly until thick and smooth. (Optional additions are 1 tablespoon of tomato purée if you want a red sauce, 2 tablespoons of crushed pineapple, or both). Add the prawns and heat for only 2 more minutes before serving.

Marmalade Duck
(Serves two)

I'm obliged to Jane Grigson for this recipe which I've adapted a little from her original. It's the classic combination of duck and orange but not in the classic way!

1 oven-ready duck
1 orange
4 oz (100 gms) marmalade (dark rather than jelly)
2 glasses water
Cress (for decoration)

Have courage; heat the oven to gas mark 6, 400°F (200°C). Place the duck in the sink and pour a kettle of boiling water over it. Pat it dry and put half the orange inside. Roast it on a rack over a dripping pan for 40 minutes. Take it out of the oven and pour away the fat from the pan. Coat the duck thoroughly with the marmalade. Pour the water into the dripping pan and put it all back in the oven for 40 minutes. Remove the duck from the oven and leave it to rest in a warm room for 10 minutes before carving. Use the water and marmalade dripping to make the sauce, adding the juice of the remaining half an orange. Decorate with cress and serve. The duck's wonderful mahogany skin and slightly sweet and sour orange flavour will never be connected with the breakfast table.

Lamb with Egg and Lemon Sauce
(Serves six)

This adaptation of the Greek *avgolemono* sauce is absolutely foolproof if you remember not to boil it. Creamy and sharp, it perfectly complements the dense but sweet flavour of lamb.

1 carrot
1 onion
Salt and pepper
1 shoulder of lamb
1 bay leaf
1 sprig thyme
Water
1 egg
Juice of 1 lemon

Peel and chop the carrot and onion and put them into an oval roasting dish or casserole. Season the lamb and place it, skin up, on the vegetables. Add the herbs and enough water to come up $\frac{1}{2}$ an inch (1 cm) around the meat. Cover the dish and cook in the oven, gas mark 4, 350°F (180°C), for 20 minutes a pound. Then remove the lamb and pour off the surplus fat, reserving the meat juices. Beat the egg and lemon juice together until frothy. Add two tablespoons of the strained lamb broth, mix well, and then pour the mixture into the rest of the broth. Heat this over a gentle heat, stirring constantly, until it thickens and coats the back of the spoon. Carve the lamb and pour a little of the sauce over each portion. Serve with rice, and the rest of the sauce in a jug.

Cod and Mushroom in Sour Cream
(Serves four)

Sour cream is much undervalued in Britain. It's much lower in fat than double cream; it has a richness just tempered by the careful souring. Fresh cream which has gone off is not the same thing! This recipe, which combines cod steaks (fresh if possible, frozen if not) with sautéd mushrooms, is a great dish if you have an oven with a timer. If everything is cool when assembled, it can be left ready to cook for up to four hours.

1 tbsp butter
4 deboned cod steaks (fresh or frozen)
8 oz (225 gms) button mushrooms
2 tbsp oil
$\frac{1}{4}$ pint (150 ml) sour cream
Juice and grated rind of 1 lemon

Lightly butter a cooking dish and put in the cod steaks. Wipe, trim and slice the mushrooms and sauté them for 3 minutes in the hot oil. Allow to cool. Beat the sour cream, the lemon juice and the grated rind together. Stir in the mushrooms and pour the mixture over the cod steaks, making sure they are completely coated. Cover with foil, bake at gas mark 6, 400°F (200°C) for 25 minutes if using fresh fish, or 35 minutes if using frozen fish. Take the foil off for the last 5 minutes to allow the sauce to brown a little. This is very good served with peas and lots of mashed potatoes.

WHITE WINES OF CHARACTER

Flavoursome sauces overpower delicate wines, white wines in particular. To stand up to the complexity of flavours, you need an assertive white wine with its own positive character. Two grape varieties notably put all their efforts into making unusually distinctive wines, the Muscat and the Gewürztraminer. Both are used in the same area of France, Alsace, and so can be found together on the same shelf in off-licences or supermarkets.

French wines are generally named after the place where the wine is made. So an area, a village, or an individual 'farm' or château may appear on the label ... and whether or not that means anything to you entirely depends on the standard of your geography, or your knowledge of wine. A happy exception is the wines of Alsace. Now you may not know where Alsace is (don't worry, many Frenchmen don't either). But that is less important than the fact that Alsace wines, which are bottled in the distinctive, extra-tall, green, flute bottle, are simply named after the grape variety used.

For the record, Alsace is a narrow stretch of land running south of Strasbourg, fringing the German border, to the far east of France. It has been a fairly constant battleground over the centuries and has been in German hands as often as French. The wines, virtually all white, reflect this in their style. They are like German wines but made by the French; fruity, but vinified to be dry.

The Muscats are very grapey, sweet-and-sour wines with a pungent, penetrating bouquet (remember eating dried muscatels?), and the Gewürztraminer grape turns its juice to the production of a rich though dry wine, full of spice. Alsace wines are still little known over here; they deserve much wider recognition, but they are gradually beginning to filter on to the supermarket shelves. They are never cheap, but for wines of their high quality, they are fairly priced and worth buying if you want a white wine of character ... with a touch of class.

Occasionally, wines are made in other parts of the world from these two grape varieties. But beware, they may sometimes be sweet. Most supermarkets and wine shops now grade their wines 1 to 9 on a dryness/sweetness scale and mark each wine accordingly on the label or the shelf. To accompany a savoury dish, a dry or medium-dry wine is best, and this will be 5 or below on the scale.

MUSHROOMS
Sherry

MUSHROOMS

Of all the free food available in Britain, the most delicious and the most ignored is the wild mushroom. People who happily pick blackberries, or even wild sorrel or sloes, avoid fungi like the plague. In other countries it's quite different. From Warsaw to Naples the arrival of autumn means the hunt is on for wild mushrooms. Aficionados have their favourite spot to which they'll return year after year. Britain is no different, except that it's rarely the British who enjoy this food for free. Expatriate Poles and Italians, and their fellow Europeans living in Britain, collect baskets of their favourite fungi each autumn in our woods. What they have conquered, and many of us haven't, perhaps wisely, is fear of eating the poisonous ones. Mushrooms which look like safe, cultivated varieties can make you quite sick. But of all the British varieties, only the Death Cap is absolutely fatal. The trick is to learn to recognise the safe ones.

Ceps (the *Boletus* family), horse mushrooms and shaggy caps, fairy-ring champignons and morels (if you are lucky enough to find them) are all safe and easily recognisable. But it is difficult to be certain of other fungi and even the most common, harmless kinds often have dangerous lookalikes. Following a good book on the subject isn't really enough to guide you; you should have at least one expedition with an expert. Your local library or council will have the address of your local natural history society, and these often run mushroom hunts. The British Mycological (fungus) Society can also help; for a list of local courses contract Dr D. W. Minter, The Foray Secretary, Commonwealth Mycological Institute, Ferry Lane, Kew, Surrey, TW9 3AF.

Why bother? Well the best of the wild mushrooms have an intensity of flavour and texture no cultivated cap ever has, despite the current move to grow more exciting kinds of mushrooms commercially. (Oyster mushrooms – flattish and strongly, though subtly, flavoured – are starting to appear in the shops in good quantities.) Shop-bought mushrooms can be used in most of these recipes; they still taste good and some can be enriched with dried wild mushrooms available from delicatessens. Dried mushrooms, when soaked, regain much of their intensity, so a little will go a long way to flavour a dish. This is a blessing when you discover the price.

Wild Mushroom Salad (from the London Hilton)
(Serves four)

1 lb (450 gms) wild mushrooms, washed but not peeled
1 chopped clove garlic
2 tbsp olive oil
1 tbsp lemon juice
$\frac{1}{2}$ tsp caster sugar
Lettuce, radishes and sorrel leaves (for the salad base)
1 tsp chopped parsley and chives

Slice the mushrooms into attractive shapes. Sauté them with the chopped garlic in 1 tablespoon of hot oil for 2 minutes. Do not let them burn. Place in a bowl and, while still warm, toss with the remaining oil, and the lemon juice mixed with the caster sugar until this has dissolved. Season, then cool. Serve on beds of shredded salad. Sprinkle with herbs, and pour on the mushroom dressing.

Mushroom Soup
(Serves four to six)

If you have only a few wild mushrooms, or mainly cultivated mushrooms and just a few dried wild fungi, this soup makes the best of them.

1 lb (450 gms) wild mushrooms (or $\frac{3}{4}$ lb (350 gms) cultivated mushrooms and 1 oz (25 gms) dried mushrooms, soaked)
1 chopped onion
2 oz (50 gms) butter
$1\frac{1}{2}$ pints (900 ml) chicken stock
2 slices white bread
5 fl oz (150 ml) single cream
Salt and pepper

Wash, trim and slice the mushrooms but don't peel them. Heat the butter and cook the onion and mushrooms over a moderate heat for 5 minutes. Add the chicken stock and simmer for 20 minutes. Cut the crusts off the bread and crumble it into the soup. Add seasoning and then liquidise or purée the soup until it is smooth. Add the cream and reheat gently. This is good served with croûtons.

Coriander Mushrooms
(Serves four)

Ceps or button mushrooms are best for this spicy version of mushrooms *à la grecque*.

1 lb (450 gms) small closed mushrooms
$\frac{1}{2}$ cup water
$\frac{1}{2}$ cup olive oil
$\frac{1}{4}$ cup lemon juice (fresh or bottled)
1 chopped clove garlic
1 tbsp chopped celery leaf (or parsley)
Salt and pepper
1 tsp ground coriander

Wash and trim the mushrooms. Bring the water, oil and lemon juice to the boil and add the mushrooms and garlic. Simmer for 5 minutes. Add the celery and season. Pour the mixture into a basin and leave to cool. Drain the mushrooms and place in a serving dish, reserving the marinade. Sprinkle the coriander over and moisten with 4 tablespoons of the marinade. Serve well-chilled.

Mushrooms Baked with Cream

This is an old country recipe that's very simple, quite delicious and can be done only with *big* mushrooms. Wild 'horse' mushrooms are the best but you can sometimes find cultivated ones over four inches across and they will do very well. It's a rich dish and is ideal for a rustic starter, or for a high tea with other country goodies.

For each person:

1 large open mushroom
2 tbsp double cream
1 tbsp butter
1 tsp parsley
Salt and pepper

Remove the stalks from the mushroom caps. Wipe and trim the caps but do not peel them. Butter a baking dish large enough to hold all the mushrooms flat and put them in, black side up. Spoon the cream on to each mushroom, with a knob of butter and generous seasoning. Bake at gas mark 7, 425°F (220°C) for 15 minutes. Sprinkle with the parsley and serve with wholemeal bread to soak up the lovely juices and cream.

Mushroom Pâté
(Serves four to six)

This is a delicious vegetarian pâté. A few wild mushrooms, or an ounce of soaked, dried ones, give the pâté a little extra flavour. It is excellent on toast, and even better served on crisp ryebread from Scandinavia.

1 lb (450 gms) mushrooms
1 small chopped onion
2 tbsp olive or sunflower oil
1 tbsp parsley
1 tbsp fresh thyme
2 tbsp butter
2 eggs
Salt and pepper

Wipe and trim the mushrooms and sauté them gently with the chopped onion in the oil for about 8 minutes, or until almost all the juice they give off has evaporated. Add the parsley and thyme and liquidise or blend in a food processor until the mixture is smooth. Using the original pan, melt the butter and scramble the eggs until well-set. Add this to the purée and blend again until smooth. Season highly and spoon into ramekins or small soufflé dishes. Chill for at least 4 hours before serving.

Mushroom and Potato Gratin
(Serves four)

This is the ultimate way of stretching mushrooms – wild or cultivated. A few wild ones will vastly improve this dish, and the combination of golden creamy potatoes and delicate earthy mushrooms seems perfect. Eat this just with hot French bread, it's far too good to serve with other strongly-flavoured food.

The dried mushrooms can be bought from good delicatessens or Chinese or Indian grocers.

$\frac{1}{4}$ pint (150 ml) boiling water
2-oz pack (50 gms) dried mushrooms
8 oz (225 gms) fresh mushrooms
2 oz (50 gms) butter
1 chopped onion
1 tsp garlic salt
1$\frac{1}{2}$ lbs (700 gms) potatoes
5 fl oz (150 ml) double cream
Grated cheese (optional)

Pour the boiling water on to the dried mushrooms and soak for 10 minutes. Wipe and trim the fresh mushrooms. Drain the dried mushrooms, reserving the water. Slice both kinds finely and fry them in the butter, together with the chopped onion and garlic salt, for 2 minutes. Peel, rinse and slice the potatoes into $\frac{1}{8}$-inch ($\frac{1}{4}$-cm) pieces and place half in a buttered baking dish. Spread the mushroom and onion mixture over the potatoes and then cover this with the remaining potatoes. Mix the mushroom water with the cream and pour it over. Top with grated cheese if desired. Bake for one hour at gas mark 4, 350°F (180°C).

SHERRY

Soup or a simple starter becomes a much more elaborate course when served with a glass of sherry. Way back, when decanters of sherry presided over the sideboard in smart dining rooms and restaurants, to tip a little into your glass – or your soup for that matter – at the start of a meal was quite the custom. The sherry was usually rich and dark – and probably off!

Sherry, like wine, has a limited life and, once the bottle is opened, gradually deteriorates. Pale, dry sherries are best finished after three weeks of opening, medium sherries after two months, and the creams after no more than six months. Decanting sherry actually hastens the decline.

Sweet sherry is made especially for the British market because until recently our taste has essentially been sweet. But in Jerez in Southern Spain near Seville, where the original sherry is made and much of it is enjoyed as well, all sherries are dry – and the more delicious for it, particularly when billed with food. Dry sherries are available in Britain as well, of course, but the range is more limited.

The most obvious type is the pale dry *Fino*, which should always be served chilled. It claims to be the driest wine in the world and by no means suits everybody. Next up the scale comes the nutty *Amontillado*, usually available as a medium sherry in Britain although it can also be found in a dry version. Even the rich, dark, sweet cream or *Oloroso* can be made dry, but regrettably this is even more of a rarity on British wine merchants' shelves.

The dry sherries are worth seeking out (ask the wine shop manager) as an unusual aperitif, or to accompany winter soup. Or you could offer your guests a choice of readily available sherries, perhaps a chilled *Fino* teamed with an *Amontillado* served at room temperature. These two sherries contrast well in taste and in appearance.

VEGETABLES
The Bottle v. the Tap:
Mineral Water

VEGETABLES

Vegetables always play a supporting role in our food. Meals are often based on meat and two veg. Waiters will say, 'Shall I bring a selection of vegetables, madam?' only *after* the meat or fish has been carefully chosen. In meat-rich Britain, this has been the pattern since medieval times when the Roast Beef of Old England became our national dish. But recently this has all been changing. There are many different factors in this change: economics, the escalating price of meat and fish; ethics – the attitudes that have created more than a million vegetarians; and health, the well-founded belief that plenty of fresh vegetables, both raw and cooked, are 'good' for you. Consequently, many people now eat more vegetables with their meat, or as a main course in their own right. Of course, these reasons ignore a crucial point: for most of us, vegetables taste good! They repay careful cooking quite as much as any choice cut of meat or delicate fillet of fish.

Methods of preparation are improving rapidly. Ten years ago cooked carrots that still had some crunch were thought undercooked, and crisp cabbage was good only for coleslaw. Nowadays, the texture is as valued as the taste, and not only on the tables of *nouvelle cuisine* chefs. I find that I often prefer the 'selection of vegetables' beautifully cooked, to the *pièce de résistance* they are supposed to accompany. At last I am working up the courage to say so, and ask for them without the 'main' dish.

The recipes here are really of two kinds: simple ways to cook fresh vegetables, and ways of using them to make whole courses on their own. Interestingly, these are not necessarily contradictory. The day when meals need neither fish nor meat but only two veg is here.

POTATOES

We often make the mistake of thinking of potatoes as just a background filler. They have a character of their own, even though few varieties actually reach the shops. As with apples, fewer varieties and standardisation are the order of the day. Only our vigorous pressure will keep even such established varieties as the King Edward from being pushed off our shelves by the tasteless, but neater-shaped, Dutch-bred potatoes. Different varieties should be cooked in different ways: waxy, firm new potatoes make wonderful salads, while others such as Maris Piper soak up much less oil when being turned into chips than alternative varieties, which may taste just the same but become fat-laden.

Potato Salad
(Serves four)

This recipe is extremely simple but can be one of the most delicious of all potato dishes if you use the *right* potatoes. They need to be small, yellow-fleshed and unblemished. The best kind which is readily available in Britain is the Jersey Royal. But if you grow your own, try to get some seed of the Pink Fir Apple as this makes an excellent salad. This is a dish to eat with the simplest of cold meats or poached fish to appreciate the full flavour of the potatoes, or on its own.

1 lb (450 gms) waxy potatoes
2 tbsp lemon juice
4 tbsp olive (or sunflower) oil
$\frac{1}{2}$ tsp sea salt
$\frac{1}{2}$ tsp fresh black pepper
1 tbsp chopped fresh chives

Scrub the potatoes and cut into equal-sized pieces. Put them in a pan with cold water and bring to the boil. Simmer until they are just tender, which will take about 10 minutes. Drain, and sprinkle them while hot with half the lemon juice. Leave to cool and then dress with the oil, remaining lemon juice and seasoning. Don't refrigerate them unless you have to. Add the chives just before serving, sprinkled on the top.

Elizabethan-style Potatoes
(Serves four)

Potatoes were thought of as an aphrodisiac in Elizabethan times when Sir Walter Raleigh first brought them back from America. They were as rare then as they are commonplace now, and this adaptation of a fancy potato pie filling shows the attention they used to get and still deserve. The mixture of sweet and sour is not at all unusual – think of apple sauce or sweet and sour prawns.

2 lbs (900 gms) potatoes (King Edwards are best)
1 oz (25 gms) butter
4 oz (100 gms) chopped onion
2 oz (50 gms) stoned dates
Salt and pepper
$\frac{1}{4}$ pint (150 ml) chicken stock (or water)
$\frac{1}{2}$ tsp ground cinnamon
$\frac{1}{2}$ tsp cloves
4 thin lemon slices

Peel the potatoes and boil for 8 minutes. Leave until cold, then cut them into walnut-sized pieces. Butter a gratin or pie dish and lay the potatoes in it. Add the onion and chopped dates. Season, pour on the chicken stock (or water), then sprinkle on the spices. Top with the lemon. Bake at gas mark 4, 350°F (180°C) for 25 minutes and serve hot on their own.

CABBAGE

Another everyday vegetable that we often take for granted is the cabbage. Khaki-coloured and soggy, it's been the butt of music-hall jokes for years. The varieties of cabbage now available are exciting: Crisp Head, Green, Chinese, Crinkly, Red and Spring – each is delicious in its own way and certainly worth the care of cooking properly. We give Anton Mosimann's cabbage recipe later in the book. Here are two of my favourites, which are particularly good in the winter when other vegetables are scarce and more expensive.

Chinese Cabbage Salad
(Serves four)

Made from the cos lettuce look-alike sold in most supermarkets as Chinese leaves, this lovely winter salad is really a splendid colour combination as well as a midwinter treat. It's a Boxing Day special in our house.

1 head Chinese leaves
2 red peppers
6 tbsp oil (preferably olive)
3 tbsp lemon juice
1 tsp sugar
$\frac{1}{2}$ tsp salt
$\frac{1}{2}$ tsp real French mustard (not the 'English French')

Cut the hard core from the cabbage and discard it. Cut the cabbage lengthwise into quarters. Slice these across (like cutting bread) into $\frac{1}{2}$-inch (1-cm) slices and crumble them into a salad bowl. Halve and deseed the peppers and cut them into $\frac{1}{8}$-inch ($\frac{1}{4}$-cm) slices across. Mix the pepper with the cabbage. Shake the dressing ingredients together in a jar, add to the salad and toss it thoroughly to blend the light-red and pale-green vegetables with the piquant dressing.

Red Cabbage with Apples
(Serves four)

This is a vegetarian winter casserole that can be served on its own or with some granary bread. In Europe, it is traditionally eaten with game like venison or hare.

$\frac{1}{2}$ head red cabbage
1 large onion
1 cooking apple
2 tbsp oil
2 tsp vinegar
2 tsp brown sugar
$\frac{1}{2}$ tsp ground cloves

Trim and chop the cabbage into $\frac{1}{2}$-inch (1-cm) slices. Peel the onion, core the apple and chop both finely. Sauté all three in the oil in a big saucepan until they glisten. Add the other ingredients and a cup of water. Cover and simmer on the lowest heat for at least 40 minutes, although leaving it for 1 hour is best. It's great reheated too!

FENNEL

Fennel is one of the exotic vegetables that are becoming commonplace in the greengrocers and on the supermarket shelves. It looks
like a sort of plump celery and that is very much its texture. But its
flavour has a subtle sweet aniseed taste that's quite different. First
an Italian way of cooking fennel (appropriately enough – they grew
it first), and second, a Chinese technique applied to a vegetable the
Chinese have probably never seen.

Stuffed Fennel

Soft cream cheese (in Italy they would use Ricotta) in fennel boats
makes a light and attractive first course, or a main course if served
in double quantitites.

Per person:

1 head fennel (or 2 small heads)
1 tsp dried oregano
$\frac{1}{2}$ lb (225 gms) cream cheese or smooth cottage cheese
4 tbsp breadcrumbs
1 tbsp olive oil
1 tbsp grated Parmesan cheese

Carefully trim the fennel and pull it apart into separate stalks. These
will look like deep spoons with short handles. Place the four largest
'bowl up' in a fireproof dish small enough to keep them stable. Mix
the herbs, cream cheese and breadcrumbs and divide into four. Place
each portion into a fennel spoon and sprinkle with oil and Parmesan
cheese. Bake in a hot oven, gas mark 5, 375°F (190°C), for 20 minutes.
Serve either hot or cold.

Stir-fry Fennel
(Serves four)

The crisp texture and aniseed flavour makes fennel an ideal candidate for Chinese-style stir frying. Have all the ingredients ready to hand before you start and cook very quickly. This dish is good either as part of a Chinese meal, or served as a vegetable with conventional lamb chops.

2 heads fennel
1 bunch spring onions
2 tbsp cooking oil
1 tsp garlic salt
2 tbsp soya sauce

Trim the fennel and onions and slice them into thin strips, keeping the white and the green parts of the onion separate. Heat a frying pan or wok, add the oil and the white parts of the onions, then the fennel. Fry on high heat for 1 minute, tossing the vegetables all the time with a spatula. Add the garlic salt and soya sauce, toss for 30 seconds more and serve sprinkled with green onion.

Cheese and Spinach Pancakes
(Serves six)

These really are a meal in their own right: a spectacular dinner-party piece that will feed six ordinary or four greedy people. If you like, cheat a little by buying some of the excellent ready-made French crêpe pancakes that are appearing in the shops. They are sold in packets of ten and are huge, 15 inches (38 cms) across, so the dish really looks astonishing.

10 pancakes, 10 inches (25 cms) or more across
2 lbs (900 gms) fresh spinach (or 1½ lbs frozen)
1 pint milk
2 oz (50 gms) cornflour
2 oz (50 gms) butter
1 tsp French Dijon mustard
8 oz (25 gms) Gruyère or Cheddar cheese
Salt and pepper
4 tbsp Parmesan cheese

Wash and cook the fresh spinach in a very little water for 5 minutes. (If using frozen spinach, defrost and heat it.) Make a cheese sauce by whisking the cornflour and butter into the cold milk and continuing to whisk regularly as you bring it to the boil. Add the mustard and Gruyère, season and heat for 2 minutes. Mix half the mixture with the spinach. On a plate at least 1 inch (2½ cms) larger than the pancakes, lay a pancake. Spread it with three dessertspoonfuls of the spinach mixture and put another pancake on top. Continue doing this, on and up, finishing with a pancake. Pour the rest of the sauce over the top and spread it as if icing a cake. Sprinkle with the Parmesan cheese and bake at gas mark 6, 400°F (200°C) for 20 minutes or until heated through and browned on top. To serve, slice the pancakes into wedges like a cake. This needs nothing with it but a fork and a healthy appetite.

THE BOTTLE V. THE TAP

It used to be thought that you couldn't get a healthier drink than a plain glass of water. That is, water from the tap. When the French first attempted to sell bottled water to the British, the marketing men might well have met their Waterloo. Pay for water, when you can get it virtually free from the tap? That would hardly be in the national character! Bottled water was considered fine for the French, but then their public source was known to be so much less reliable.

In Britain, with one of the safest water supplies in the world, it hardly seemed necessary. Or did it? Obviously the Great British Public believed it was. The bottled water market is now worth about £40 million a year, and we are prepared to pay nearly as much for a bottle of the stuff as we are for a litre of petrol.

And it's not just a passing fad. Although water supplies in Britain are still safe, some now seem rather less appetising than they might be. Take London, for instance, where at least a third of the tap water supply is 'treated sewage effluent', hardly a phrase to be conjured with, let alone drunk.

In many parts of the country, water from the tap contains not only essential minerals, but undesirable chemicals as well. A glass of water has gradually become less and less 'healthy'. People have turned instead to the bottle and sales of spa, spring, well, mineral – call it what you will – water have boomed as a result. But how do you know that what you are paying for is any better than water from the tap? Where did all these different bottled waters suddenly spring from, and how safe are the sources?

Well, Health Authorities make sure that water for sale is wholesome to drink. But, like tap water, this wholesomeness is in some cases acquired by treatment. Not all waters are equally naturally pure. Until mid-1985, there was nothing to differentiate one bottle from another in terms of quality. Now, however, there are some words you can look for on the label that guarantee the water is 'naturally microbiologically wholesome' (that is, it does not have to be disinfected in any way) and has passed a number of very stringent tests.

Natural Mineral Water, and that is precisely how it is described, has to come from a protected source and be naturally wholesome and pure; it may not be treated in any way. A number of French waters have earned the right to use this label, as well as some British ones. Two to look out for which are widely available and already display the new appellation on their labels are Highland Spring and Sainsbury's.

Other bottled waters, which may be called anything other than natural mineral water, are still much more pleasant-tasting than common or garden tap water, and much better-looking too. When doing a tasting of unlabelled waters for the *Food and Drink* programme, we could actually pick out the tap water on sight; against the others it looked slightly yellow. But remember that as far as the law is concerned, these other bottled waters need only meet the same requirements as water from the tap.

RICE

Lager

RICE

Rice is thought by many to be the cereal of the 1980s. It's low in fat and gives rise to few, if any, allergies. It's cheap, easy to store and is proving steadily more and more popular in Britain, both in its natural form and in the wide variety of prepared flavoured versions that can be found everywhere. Raise the subject of the best method of cooking rice among a group of cooks and you will have a major controversy on your hands. But there's no one method that's best. It's not realised often enough how excitingly varied rice can be in shape, method of cooking, flavour and texture. This sheer variety was demonstrated for us when a number of New Britons from many different parts of the world showed us their ways of cooking rice. Whether they came from Italy or China, India or Basingstoke, they had their own favourite variety of rice and method of cooking it. The same rice, for instance, cooked by a Chinese or an Indian cook would come out differently, because the former might want to eat it with chopsticks and therefore would make it stick together, while the latter would eat it with a spoon and would therefore want it dry and fluffy.

Here are some of the varieties of rice:

Pudding rice: this is the sort we are most used to. It is a short-grained rice, originally from the Carolinas in America, whose special quality is to cook until totally soft while absorbing enormous amounts of liquid.

Brown rice: all rice has comparatively little fibre, but brown rice has more than most. It consists of the unpolished rice grain and takes longer to cook than white rice. It has a nutty flavour.

Long-grain: this is a polished rice with a long, thin shape often called Patna or Indian rice, depending on where it was grown. It makes a good background to Chinese and other spicy food, and forms the base for pilaus and birianis. The best, most expensive and most flavourful among the long-grains is Basmati, which is grown exclusively in the Indian subcontinent.

Italian or Arborio rice: this is medium-grain rice which has a plump look. A great absorber of liquids and flavours, it's particularly famous for the Italian risotto dishes.

Pre-fluffed, 'Uncle Ben' type rice: rice with this description has already been steam-cooked, and will absorb more water and expand to a greater size when cooked than raw rice. It isn't quicker to cook but it is more foolproof. It's often used in America and the West Indies.

Sour Cream and Orange Rice
(Serves four to six)

1½ pints (900 ml) water
1 dash lemon juice
1 dash good-quality soya sauce
1 lb (450 gms) long-grain brown rice
4 tbsp oil and lemon dressing
1 medium red pepper, deseeded and chopped
2 sticks celery, chopped
4 oz (100 gms) black raisins
4 oz (100 gms) toasted cashew nuts
4 oz (100 gms) lentil sprouts or any seasonal vegetable
1 bunch spring onions, chopped
3 medium oranges, peeled and segmented
½ pint (300 ml) sour cream
Salt and pepper

Bring the water to the boil in a saucepan, adding the lemon juice and soya sauce. Meanwhile, rinse the rice in cold water to remove any dirt or grains of starch. Add the rice to the saucepan and bring back to the boil. Reduce the heat until the water is simmering, and put a tight-fitting lid on the saucepan. Simmer for 25 minutes without removing the lid. Turn off the heat and leave the rice in the saucepan for a further 5 minutes before taking off the lid. Add the oil and lemon dressing while the rice is still hot.

Leave the rice to cool and then stir in all the other ingredients, reserving some orange segments for decoration. Season, and decorate the salad with the reserved orange pieces and the sour cream.

Chinese Boiled Rice using Long-Grain Rice
(Serves six)

Cooking the rice in the Chinese way helps it stick together slightly which makes it easier to pick up with chopsticks. This is the base of all Chinese rice dishes.

1 lb (450 gms) long-grain rice

Wash the rice and put into a saucepan. Add an equal volume of water and bring to the boil. Boil steadily until all the water has been absorbed. Turn down heat to minimum and, using a heat diffuser to ensure the rice does not burn, leave for 15 minutes. The rice will then be ready to serve.

Chinese Fried Rice
(Serves three to four)

This is a dish compiled from pre-cooked ingredients. It's pretty, delicious and quick to cook. Don't be tempted to add anything else that's been left in the refrigerator – the balance of colour and texture is quite important.

2 tbsp oil
4 oz (100 gms) chopped onion
4 oz (100 gms) green peas (fresh or frozen)
6 oz (175 gms) peeled prawns
2 eggs
8 oz (225 gms) rice, cooked as above and cooled
$\frac{1}{2}$ tbsp soya sauce

Heat the oil in a large pan. Sauté the onion for 2 minutes, then add the peas and prawns and fry for a further minute. Beat the eggs, add them to the pan and scramble them until dry. Add the rice and stir until it is heated through and golden. Serve sprinkled with soya sauce. With a bowl of soup, this makes a complete meal.

Risotto alla Milanese
(Serves four to six)

Italian risottos are made by cooking their own unusual rice in a special way. The final texture of the dish is crucial; it should be slightly moist or even creamy, and each grain should be separate with just a little bite. Don't stint on the saffron as it makes all the difference.

1 pinch saffron
2 pints (1 litre) beef stock
3 oz (75 gms) butter
1 small chopped onion
$\frac{1}{2}$ glass dry white wine
12 oz (350 gms) Arborio rice
4 oz (100 gms) grated Parmesan cheese

Steep the saffron in 2 tablespoons of warmed stock for 5 minutes or so. Heat half the butter in a heavy pan, add the chopped onion and cook until it is very light yellow in colour. Add the wine, followed by the rice, stirring constantly with a wooden spoon until it is blended thoroughly.

Pour in the stock gradually, stirring frequently as the rice thickens. After 10 minutes, add the saffron and grated Parmesan cheese. When the rice has a transparent appearance, the risotto is ready. Add the remaining butter, stir well and serve immediately.

Chicken Pilau Rice using Basmati Rice
(Serves four to six)

Variations of this chicken dish are cooked from Istanbul to the Burmese border, and perhaps beyond into Malaysia. This version comes from the Afghan foothills. It's golden, savoury and a good party dish, especially if you sprinkle it with 2 oz (50 gms) of crisp, salted almonds just before serving.

1 chicken cut in joints
1 tbsp oil or clarified butter
1 large chopped onion
1 peeled and crushed clove garlic
2 bay leaves
1 or 2 cinnamon sticks
8 oz (225 gms) Basmati rice
$\frac{3}{4}$ pint (450 ml) chicken stock
1 pinch saffron
Salt and pepper

Fry the chicken in the oil or clarified butter until it is brown. Add the onion and garlic, spices and rice and stir until the rice is translucent. Add the chicken stock steadily until the pan stops sizzling (using approximately twice the volume of stock to the rice). Season, and stir well, then cover and simmer for 30 minutes. Then dilute the saffron in 1 tablespoon of hot water and dribble it over the top of the dish. Replace the lid and cook for a further 10 minutes. Remove the cinnamon before serving.

Caribbean Rice and Peas
(Serves three to four)

The national dish of Jamaica, this combines red kidney beans (known as peas) with coconut milk and rice to make a spicy mixture which is traditionally eaten with chicken fricassee.

$\frac{1}{2}$ 15-oz tin red kidney beans (or 4 oz (100 gms) dried beans, soaked and cooked)
8 oz (225 gms) rice
$\frac{3}{4}$ pint (450 ml) water
1 sprig of thyme
1 dried chilli
Salt and pepper
2 oz (50 gms) creamed coconut

If you are not using tinned kidney beans, soak the beans overnight and boil them in plenty of water for 45 to 50 minutes, making sure they boil vigorously for at least 10 minutes. Bring the rice, water, seasonings and creamed coconut to the boil. Add the kidney beans, cover and simmer on the lowest heat until all the liquid has evaporated and the rice is cooked. This will take about 30 minutes.

LAGER

Beer is usually a better accompaniment to ethnic dishes than wine, when you need a long drink to quench your thirst. Lager is the ideal beer for the table but, sad to say, the best choice is not always British. Our home-brewed lager beers generally have less character, less maturity and less alcohol than those from abroad.

The laws governing customs and excise duty discourage British brewers from making lagers properly. Since tax is paid by the brewers in advance of sale, economically it is in their interests to send out lager as quickly as possible, leaving it little time to mature or 'condition'. (The word lager, incidentally, actually means to condition.) French and German brewers who do not have to carry this financial burden, on the other hand, can afford to do the job properly.

Looking closely at a bottle or can, an identifiable indication of quality is the alcohol content of a beer, and this is generally expressed on the label in terms of original gravity; the lower the original gravity, the poorer the quality. (Original gravity reflects the quantity of sugar present before fermentation and this accords with the amount of alcohol that will be generated. 1030 means slightly less than 3% alcohol, 1040 less than 4% and so on. A good lager would not be less than 1045 or 4.5%; strong lager starts at 1050.) Typical supermarket canned lagers in Britain are among the weakest in the world, if they were any weaker they would not be entitled to the name beer.

As well as revealing the original gravity and so the strength and the quality, the label on a bottle or can of lager will also state where the beer is brewed. Frequently, lagers that appear to be imported from abroad are in fact brewed under licence over here, and so suffer from the same shortcomings as our own home-brewed beers. Needless to say, not every lager brewed in this country is a disappointment; there are exceptions to every rule. Many small breweries around Britain genuinely care about the quality of their beers. But, generally speaking, better lagers are brewed in Germany, France, Holland and Belgium than in the UK.

APPLES
Liquid Gold:
Cider and Apple Juice

APPLES

In Britain, although we grow nearly eighty varieties of eating and cooking apples, only two or three varieties ever seem to reach the shops. This is partly our own fault – we don't know which varieties to ask for or when they are in season. It's also partly the fault of the supermarkets and greengrocers who only too often bulk-buy just one or two varieties to a set standard and price.

Over the last five years a determined marketing effort, led by the French in particular, has transformed apple sales in this country. The crisp texture, mild taste and reliability of the French Golden Delicious has earned it dominance in the shops. This is best when eaten *golden*, as the French do, and not anaemic green as we tend to. But for complex subtle flavours and a balance between sharpness and sweetness the English apples are unmatched. The *Food and Drink* programme tasted twenty-three kinds, from an old-fashioned monster called Bloody Ploughman to the modern crossbreeds such as Greensleeves.

The apples raised in Britain in the nineteenth century (like Cox's and the less well-known but equally delicious Blenheim Orange and Ribston Pippins) came out as the favourites. Of course, Cox's are still widely available and much loved. As for the others, only *we* can bring them back by demanding them regularly. This will make it economically sensible for the supermarkets and greengrocers to stock them.

If you want to try some of the more unusual apples we looked at and tasted, we've listed a few below. Why not ask for them by name and continue to bully your local shop till it gets them in? As an alternative, the English Tourist Board has a leaflet listing dozens of varieties and the farms that grow them across the country. It's obtainable from the Farm Shop Association, Hunger Lane, Mugginton, Derby, DE6 4PL.

Some seasonal varieties to look for include:

Early season, Beauty of Bath, Discovery, Worcester Pearmain, Ellison's Orange

Mid-season, Charles Ross, Blenheim Orange, Egremont Russet, Sunset

Late season, Ribston Pippin, Jonathan, Laxton's Superb, Kidd's Orange Red, Ashmead's Kernel.

And for a final tip, why not try a French idea and cook with what we think of as eating apples. Lots of the recipes below benefit from the scented flavour of dessert apples whose firm flesh doesn't disintegrate as easily as the cookers'.

Baked Apple Meringue
(Serves four)

This recipe is served in one of the most highly commended restaurants in Britain where it costs over £7 per portion. It's easy to make, much cheaper and just as good at home!

4 large Cox's apples
4 dsp sultanas
4 dsp soft brown sugar
1 tsp ground cinnamon
1 cup apple juice
1 egg white
$\frac{1}{2}$ tsp cider vinegar
2 tbsp caster sugar

Core the apples without piercing the base. Scoop out the top of each apple and fill with a dessertspoon each of sultanas and soft brown sugar. Sprinkle with cinnamon and place the apples into a baking dish with the apple juice. Whisk the egg white until stiff and add half a teaspoon of cider vinegar. Fold in the caster sugar and beat until smooth. Top each apple with a quarter of the meringue mixture and bake at gas mark 4, 350°F (180°C) for 45 minutes.

Apple Jacques Pancakes
(Serves four)

This is one of the most popular tea-time recipes I know and is extremely easy. It's derived from a Normandy recipe and takes about as long to make as to read the instructions. The pancakes are fabulous served with lemon, honey or sugar, and are stupendous with apricot jam.

8 oz (225 gms) apples
1 tbsp lemon juice
1 egg
1 tbsp oil
8 oz (225 gms) plain flour
$\frac{1}{2}$ pint (300 ml) milk to mix

Grate the unpeeled apples and mix with the lemon juice. Beat the egg, oil and flour together and blend in the milk until the mixture is as smooth and thick as single cream. This usually takes about $\frac{1}{2}$ pint (300 ml) of milk, but may vary according to the flour used. Stir in the apples. Drop the mixture in tablespoonfuls on to a hot greased griddle or frying pan. Each tablespoonful will form a thick $2\frac{1}{2}$-inch (6-cm) pancake. Turn the pancakes after 2 minutes and cook for another 90 seconds or so. Serve hot with apricot jam, honey, sugar or lemon.

Pheasant with Apples
(Serves four)

Normandy, like Kent, also specialises in growing apples. A traditional Norman French dish is pheasant (or chicken or guinea-fowl), cooked with apples and cream. Deliciously rich, it's also surprisingly economical – cooked in this way, a pheasant will easily serve four.

This is a low-fat version but if you want true authenticity and don't mind high cholesterol, omit the cornflour and use double cream.

1 pheasant, cleaned and jointed into four pieces
2 tbsp butter
1 chopped onion
Bouquet garni (celery, bay leaf, parsley and thyme)
$\frac{1}{2}$ pint (300 ml) apple juice
Salt and pepper
2 eating apples, preferably Cox's or Blenheims
$\frac{1}{4}$ pint (150 ml) single cream
1 tbsp cornflour

Sauté the pheasant pieces in a tablespoonful of butter until lightly browned. Put them into a casserole together with the chopped onion and the bouquet garni. Heat the apple juice in the browning pan until bubbling and pour it over the pheasant. Add the seasoning and either simmer on a low heat or bake in the oven at gas mark 4, 350°F (180°C) for 40 minutes. Core and slice the apples but don't peel them, then sauté in the remaining butter. Blend together the cream and cornflour and add this and the apples to the casserole. Bring to the boil and simmer until thick and the apples are hot. Serve with plain mashed potatoes or rice.

Waldorf Salad
(Serves three to four)

This salad is said to have been invented at the Waldorf Astoria hotel in New York at the beginning of this century. It could be true as the Americans have a gift for 'meal' salads that's second to none. When made with chicken, this is a main course. But for vegetarians, or to go with a cold table, it is still very good without the chicken.

2 crisp apples of contrasting colours
1 head of celery
4 oz (100 gms) walnut halves
8 oz (225 gms) cooked chicken breast
Juice of $\frac{1}{2}$ a lemon
Salt and pepper
$\frac{1}{4}$ pint (150 ml) mayonnaise (home-made or a good-quality commercial brand)

Core, but don't peel, the apples and cut them into $\frac{1}{2}$-inch (1-cm) chunks. Wash the inner stalks of the celery and cut them into similar-sized pieces. Chop the walnut pieces in half, saving some for decoration. Slice the chicken. Mix the apples, celery, walnuts and chicken with the lemon juice. Season the mixture and add the mayonnaise. Stir well and chill for 30 minutes. Serve in lettuce cups decorated with walnut halves and celery leaves.

Apple Cake
(Serves four to six)

More a pudding than a cake, this dish comes originally from Sweden but has been adapted all over the world. It resembles a cold version of our apple crumble, but it's spicier and more exotic. Served without cream, it makes a refreshing end to a rich winter meal.

2 lb (900 gms) cooking apples
8 oz (225 gms) brown sugar
$\frac{1}{2}$ tsp ground cinnamon
$\frac{1}{2}$ tsp ground cloves
1 lb (450 gms) fresh brown breadcrumbs (these can be made in a blender or food processor)

Peel, core and slice the apples and cook them with 6 oz (175 gms) of the sugar until soft and translucent. Stir in the spices and leave to cool. Mix the breadcrumbs with the remaining 2 oz (50 gms) of sugar and bake for 15 minutes in a coolish oven, gas mark 2, 300°F (150°C). Allow the breadcrumb mixture to cool. Divide the two separate mixtures into 3 parts each and place them in layers in a bowl, starting with apple and finishing with crumbs. Use a glass bowl if possible, to show off the layers. Chill for 2 hours in a refrigerator. The contrasts of texture and flavour are really intriguing.

Apple and Spice Yoghurt
(Serves four)

This dish is as nice at breakfast as at dinner. For grand occasions, serve it in wineglasses – it looks very appetising. If you don't make your own yoghurt, buy one of the whole milk or goat's milk varieties now available.

4 eating apples
1 oz (25 gms) white sugar
1 tsp ground cinnamon
$\frac{1}{2}$ tsp ground cloves
2 oz (50 gms) crystallised ginger
2 oz (50 gms) fine oatmeal
1 pint (600 ml) plain yoghurt
4 tsp honey (optional)

Peel, core and dice the apples. Simmer them with the sugar, spices and a little (2 tablespoons) of water until they are soft and translucent, but not puréed. Leave to cool. Toast the oatmeal under a grill until golden and allow to cool. Mix the apples and yoghurt together. Chill for 2 hours. Serve sprinkled with oatmeal and perhaps a teaspoon of runny honey on each portion.

LIQUID GOLD: CIDER AND APPLE JUICE

The apple is not just in legend a magic fruit – the crop of the blessed tree of immortality – but is also the inspiration for real-life alchemists. There are pots of gold to be made both from fermenting apples and turning them into cider, and also from selling still or sparkling apple juice. Cider, the traditional British drink, was for centuries drunk only down on the farm and had an unfashionable image. But it has finally shaken the straw from its flagon and relaunched itself into society in sleek, foil-crowned bottles to win over sophisticated drinkers.

The clear, bright, frequently fizzy, alcoholically-subdued drink calling itself cider today has, however, lost a great deal of its original character. To make every batch reliably consistent and stable enough to travel great distances and endure a long shelf-life, revolutionary methods of production have had to be introduced. Now not only is foreign apple (and even occasionally pear) concentrate used in our British ciders, but the brew itself is also tampered with. Instead of being a living product, like wine or real ale, most cider today has been killed and sterilised.

There is an enormous difference between the commercial brands of Strongbow or Blackthorn, for instance, and the powerful brews doled out earlier this century as part of farm labourers' pay. And just as well, you might say. Scrumpy has rather a rotten reputation nowadays: rumour has it that it sends you mad (or at least upsets your stomach). In fact traditional cider, made simply from the naturally fermented juice of apples, is a very individual and delicious drink.

In the traditional cider-producing areas of England, notably the West Country, natural farm cider can still be bought by the roadside on any tourist route. It is cloudy, pungent and can be surprisingly bitter and tart. Good cider-makers who use the right sort of cider apples (there are hundreds of varieties to choose from, including the delightfully-named Slack-my-Girdle and Handsome Maud) and who follow the traditional cider-making methods can make ciders of infinite complexity and variety. For the record, cider apples are certainly not a treat to eat. One bite and your lips pucker like a prune and your tongue feels as though you've just sucked a lemon.

Traditional cider is very dry, and either still or just slightly sparkling. Whether the brew is cloudy or clear, it will have quite a bit of body and will leave a bittersweet sensation on the tongue. It is usually stronger than Guinness and often almost as alcoholic as white wine, so beware!

Inch's Cider Company in Winkleigh, Devon, is probably the largest scrumpy-maker in Europe. Arguably the best of their range is the dry, traditional scrumpy which is available in a stone jar as well as in ordinary litre bottles or on draught. This is very light but surprisingly acidic; its clean taste disguises its strength.

East Anglia has become another important region for producing real cider. The contrasting styles of Elmham House and Aspall ciders are highly recommended. Elmham House is produced by a brave English winemaker, Robin Donn. One year, a disastrous hailstorm wrecked his vineyards, so he decided to press his Cox's apples in the wine press instead. The result was a very refined cider, really an apple wine. This is pale, still and dry and at 8% alcohol is in fact nearer in strength, taste and presentation to wine than cider. Aspall cider is a much earthier product and is made by following the cider traditions of centuries – the Aspall cider company was actually formed in 1718. The brew is dark and heavy, with an intense smell and taste of apples. It can best be described as a sort of alcoholic apple juice. And, fittingly, like other genuine ciders, it is found in licensed health food shops. Both these ciders complement food excellently, especially salads and dishes of ham and pork.

The taste for apples is firmly established now and several refreshing, light, non-alcoholic apple drinks have recently elbowed their way into the market. Made from pure apple juice, with bubbles being the only additive, they are highly recommendable in almost every way . . . except for the fact that they are made from the juice of foreign apples. Britain grows the best apples in the world and makes the most cider as well. But the two are not so closely linked as you might expect since, perversely, the new alchemy which turns apples into highly-fashionable drinks is transforming more foreign than British orchards into gold-mines.

CHRISTMAS COOKING
Celebration Fizz

CHRISTMAS COOKING

Christmas comes but once a year . . . so goes the over-quoted rhyme. But, gastronomically, perhaps it's just as well. Apart from the predictable way we over-indulge in it, most traditional Christmas food has two other disadvantages: it's unhealthy, consisting of quantities of saturated fats and sugars, little or no fibre or raw food (turkey may be lean but how often is it seen without sausagemeat or bacon?); second, Christmas food gets boring – turkey hot, turkey cold, turkey in the fridge five days old! Khaki-coloured sprouts won't do even in soup the third time round, and those suet-based puddings and solid cakes start to drag by Boxing Day. So *Food and Drink's* Christmas took on a new look. We experimented with healthier, easier ways of cooking the turkey; some surprising, though old-fashioned, ways of using up the leftovers; and some unusual vegetable recipes into the bargain. Perhaps most successful of all, we made a Christmas pudding and a Christmas cake that contain no added fats at all, but are as dark, rich and moist (and even more delicious) than their suety siblings. And remember, many of these recipes are perfectly good on their own at other times of the year.

Crafty Turkey Roasting

Roasting a turkey is so often a matter of guesswork. To get the legs properly cooked while keeping the breast moist isn't always easy. Well, there is a crafty way of doing this which makes the gravy at the same time. But first, just a few points about defrosting and stuffing a turkey. If the bird is frozen, defrost it *out* of the fridge for at least forty-eight hours before Christmas Day. If you are not going to stuff it in the traditional way, place an apple and a lemon inside for flavour. If you must stuff it, try not to use sausagemeat. This takes so long to cook through that the outside of the bird can be cooked to ribbons before the stuffing is ready. White or brown breadcrumbs, herbs and lemon rind, bound together with two eggs, make a delicious stuffing. Now for the crafty bit.

Put the turkey on a rack *over* the roasting tin. Pour one pint of water into the tin under it. Cover the breast loosely with buttered foil and roast at gas mark 4, 350°F (180°C) for sixteen minutes to the pound for turkeys up to ten pounds in weight; and for fourteen minutes to the pound for turkeys over ten pounds. Don't forget to include the weight of the stuffing when calculating the roasting time. After cooking, remove the foil and leave the turkey in a warm place to rest for twenty minutes. Meanwhile, pour off the ready-made gravy, containing all the cooking juices, from the pan and get the trimmings ready. The bird will be delicious, moist and cooked through.

Make your own cranberry sauce to accompany it; nothing could be easier. This version has a delicate tang of orange zest. In the unlikely event of your having any left over, it will keep for months in a jar in the refrigerator.

Cranberry Sauce

1 lb (450 gms) cranberries (fresh or bottled)
Juice and grated rind of 1 orange
6 oz (175 gms) caster sugar

Put the cranberries and the orange juice into a saucepan and bring to the boil. Cover the pan and simmer for 10 minutes (the cranberries will pop!). Add the sugar and grated orange rind, and stir until the sugar is dissolved. Simmer for a further 10 minutes. Decant into jars and cool before serving.

Parson
(Serves three)

This traditional dish was inspired by the spices that were beginning to arrive in Britain from India at the end of the eighteenth century. It has an original spicy flavour which makes a welcome antidote to the tedium of endless cold cuts. Serve with moulded rice and mango chutney.

8 oz (225 gms) rice
1 chopped onion
1 level tbsp mild curry powder
1 tbsp butter
1 tbsp flour
$\frac{1}{2}$ pint (300 ml) milk
8 oz (225 gms) cold cooked turkey, cut into cubes
1 tbsp olive oil
1 tbsp chopped fresh parsley

Boil the rice until cooked, drain and keep it hot. Meanwhile, fry the onion with the curry powder in melted butter for 2 minutes. Stir in the flour and add the milk gradually. Whisk to a smooth sauce. Simmer for 5 minutes and then add the turkey, and heat through.

Grease a ring mould with olive oil. Sprinkle some chopped parsley on the bottom of the mould and then add the cooked rice. Press it down firmly and cover the mould with a plate. Turn it upside down, give the mould a sharp tap and turn the rice out on to a serving plate. Fill the centre with the 'Parson' and serve immediately.

Christmas Vegetables

Vegetables are always a problem with Christmas cooking as everyone expects Brussels sprouts and potatoes but gets bored with them very quickly. Here is a slightly unusual way with sprouts: some Christmassy chestnuts have been added to give them crunch. Dried chestnuts, which can be used as an alternative to fresh chestnuts, are available from health food shops.

Here are also some alternatives to potatoes – celeriac, a vegetable with a celery taste and the looks of a lumpy turnip; and Jerusalem artichokes, with the appearance of knobbly potatoes but a nutty flavour. Both dishes are tasty enough to be eaten on their own.

Sprouts and Chestnuts
(Serves four)

4 oz (100 gms) chestnuts (fresh or dried)
1 lb (450 gms) Brussels sprouts
2 oz (50 gms) butter
Black pepper

If you are using dried chestnuts, soak them for 2 hours and then boil them for 10 minutes. If you are using fresh chestnuts, first drop them into boiling water for 30 seconds. Then remove them and slit the skins. Replace them in boiling water for a further 30 seconds. Remove them again and they should slip out of their skins. Cook them by simmering for 20 minutes.

Meanwhile, boil the sprouts in the normal way; keeping them crisp and light-green. Then finely chop them, or purée in a food processor, adding the butter and plenty of black pepper. Serve the purée hot with the cooked chestnuts. The purée has a surprisingly delicate taste and has a lovely fresh-green colour.

Jerusalem Artichokes Provençal
(Serves four)

1 lb (450 gms) Jerusalem artichokes
1 tbsp oil (preferably olive oil)
1 small chopped onion
$\frac{1}{2}$ tsp garlic salt
8 oz (225 gms) tinned tomatoes

Peel and slice the artichokes. Heat the oil in a frying pan and stir in the artichokes, making sure they are coated in hot oil. Add the onion, garlic salt and tomatoes. Stir well and cook gently for 10 to 15 minutes, until the artichokes are cooked.

Celeriac
(Serves four)

1 celeriac
$\frac{1}{2}$ oz (15 gms) butter
$\frac{1}{2}$ oz (15 gms) flour
$\frac{1}{2}$ pint (300 ml) milk
2 tbsp breadcrumbs
2 tbsp Parmesan cheese

Dice and peel the celeriac and parboil it for 6 to 7 minutes. While this is cooking, melt the butter in a pan, add the flour and mix well. Add the milk gradually, stirring all the time over a medium heat until the sauce is smooth and glossy. Keep hot over a gentle heat until the celeriac finishes cooking. Drain this, then add it to the white sauce. Pour it into a gratin dish, making sure the celeriac is covered with sauce. Sprinkle the Parmesan cheese and breadcrumbs over the top. Bake in the oven for 30 minutes at gas mark 4, 350°F (180°C), or until the topping is brown and crispy.

A *Food and Drink* tradition which also took place at Christmas was a consumer tasting-test. This time we looked at shop-bought Christmas puddings for those who missed the Stir-up Sunday programme, on which the *Food and Drink* Christmas pudding had also been featured. For those who like to make their own, the Crafty Christmas Pudding recipe is included here, but for anyone who won't get around to it, the best of the nine shop-bought puddings were the National Trust pudding, Prewett's wholemeal pudding and Mrs Peake's pudding. The best value for money was Mrs Peake's.

Crafty Christmas Pudding
(Serves four)

This recipe was devised by a French chef in the 1920s. Unorthodox in many ways, it is dark, rich and fruity. It has become a firm family favourite.

1 lb (450 gms) wholemeal breadcrumbs
8 oz (225 gms) currants
8 oz (225 gms) sultanas
4 oz (100 gms) grated apples, including the peel
4 oz (100 gms) chopped bananas
4 oz (100 gms) chopped Brazil nuts
8 oz (225 gms) soft brown sugar
Juice and rind of 1 lemon
3 tsp mixed spice
1 oz (25 gms) chopped almonds
3 eggs
$\frac{1}{2}$ pint (300 ml) milk
1 tsp salt

Mix together all the ingredients and stir well. Put the mixture into a buttered pudding basin. The quantities given make enough for one 4-pint basin, or two 2-pint basins. Cover with greaseproof paper, securing it with an elastic band. Steam for 3 hours and then allow to cool. Store in a cool place until Christmas Day and then steam for 1 hour before serving in the traditional way. It's best made at least three weeks before eating.

Fruit and Nut Christmas Cake

To round off the festivities, here is a recipe for a fabulous Christmas cake so full of fruit and nuts there's hardly any room left for cake! It is so rich that it's best made in a ring mould so it can be sliced thinly. Not only does it taste good, but the multi-coloured glacé cherries make it look as though it contains jewels.

5 oz (150 gms) whole Brazil nuts
5 oz (150 gms) halved walnuts
5 oz (150 gms) whole almonds
4 oz (100 gms) dried apricots
4 oz (100 gms) chopped dried dates
6 oz (175 gms) mixed glacé cherries
3 oz (75 gms) raisins
3 oz (75 gms) candied peel
Grated rind and juice of 1 lemon
3 oz (75 gms) sifted plain flour
$\frac{1}{2}$ tsp salt
$\frac{1}{2}$ tsp baking powder
1 tsp vanilla essence
3 oz (75 gms) soft brown sugar
3 eggs

Mix all the fruit and nuts together. In a separate large bowl whisk together all the other ingredients to make a smooth batter. Add the nuts and fruit to the batter and stir well until they are all covered and bound together.

Line and grease an 8-inch (20-cm) cake tin and pour in the cake mixture. Bake for 2 hours at gas mark 2, 300°F (150°C).

This cake can be made up to three days before Christmas and will keep for three months in a cake tin.

Mulled Cider

Here is a vintage recipe for a cider cup and a century-old recipe for marrow rum which Jill Goolden collected for our Exmoor Christmas party. Cider makes a delicious winter warmer, spiced up a bit and served hot. For children, apple juice can be used instead. Both go as well with food as on their own. For each mug of medium-sweet cider or apple juice allow:

5 berries whole allspice
2 cloves
$\frac{1}{4}$ stick cinnamon (broken off lengthways)
$\frac{1}{2}$ tsp sugar, mixed with a little powered cinnamon

Place all ingredients, except the sugar and powered cinnamon, in a pan over a medium heat and allow to infuse without boiling for at least 10 minutes. Strain the liquid into heat-proof glasses or mugs and sprinkle with the cinnamon sugar. If large quantities are being made, an orange can be pierced with the cloves and baked in a low oven for about 30 minutes before being floated in the infusing liquid.

Marrow Rum

This is a quaint nineteenth-century recipe. It is fun to make and surprisingly good to taste. It is best made months before Christmas to allow it sufficient time to mature.

1 large ripe marrow
Enough demerara sugar to fill the marrow cavity
$\frac{1}{2}$ tsp dried general-purpose wine yeast
2 tbsp warm water
Juice of 1 orange
Handful of raisins (optional)

The marrow should be ripe, but must have a tough, hard skin. Cut the stalk end off about 4 inches (10 cms) down. Scoop out the pith and seeds. Pack the cavity with the sugar. Follow the directions on the packet of dried yeast to activate it and then mix it with the warm water and orange juice. Pour this over the sugar into the marrow, keeping it upright, of course. Replace the top and seal well with adhesive tape. Place the marrow inside a nylon stocking (or one side of a pair of tights) and suspend it upright in a warm place. Alternatively, stand it in a jug. After about three weeks, the liquid inside will begin to seep out. At this stage, puncture the marrow and allow the juice to run into a fermentation jar with an airlock. If you are adding raisins, place them in this jar before sealing it. When the fermentation has finished (this will take approximately two weeks, but is very variable), rack the liquid off the sediment into clean, sterilised bottles and store. The longer it has to mature, the better it will be.

CELEBRATION FIZZ

Sparkling wine is the supreme celebration drink, and around Christmas and New Year there are more excuses for buying a bottle than at most other times of the year. But not being a regular passenger in the supermarket trolley, sparkling wine is a bit of an unknown quantity. People shop for it in the dark, feeling their way around on the price tags. Much more than simple pounds and pence distinguishes one bottle from another, however. A huge chasm divides one well-made, well-matured bottle of fizz which will be refreshing and delicious to drink from another that can taste tart, acidic and raw. Fizz is still considered a luxury and, when buying a luxury, you certainly don't want to be disappointed.

Champagne is the most famous, most expensive sparkling wine and is also the best. For many of us, most champagnes are too expensive for all but the most special of celebrations, although supermarkets have done their best to cut the price. In so doing, they have also shaved the quality. Supermarket champagnes are usually just too young and too raw to be that much of a luxury; the best way to take advantage of their lower prices is to buy them well ahead of time and allow them to age a bit at home, laying them on their sides in a cool, dark corner. Cheap champagnes will continue to improve in the bottle for anything up to three years.

The expense of champagne depends on many factors, including the method used to put the bubbles in the wine. The costly *méthode champenoise* is also used for other good sparkling wines, and in itself is something of a guarantee of quality. If used, it will almost certainly be boasted on the label so this is something to look out for.

Some of the best alternatives to champagne are the sparkling wines of Saumur, on the Loire in France. These are light, fresh, generally dry wines which are all made by the painstaking champagne method. As well as the well-known names (Gratien & Meyer is the most famous), there are cheaper supermarket own-labels as well. These may be too astringently dry for some tastes; slightly sweeter styles are marked on the label as *Demi Sec*.

Spain has a family of sparkling wines following (as best they can) the champagne tradition. Cava is the family title and finding this on a bottle of sparkling wine is another sort of guarantee. Most Cavas (Freixenet, for example) come from the Barcelona area and are rather softer and more 'soupy' as a result of the hot sun.

'Sekt' means sparkling wine in German, but do not be confused; it does *not* mean German sparkling wine. Most Sekts are made by a bulk process from the cheapest white wines siphoned off the European wine lake, and then made sparkling in Germany. They are almost all inferior products far removed from luxury, and deserve to be given a wide berth. An exception are the Sekts made from the riesling grape, which offer a delicious, individual, floral flavour, and so this is worth looking for on the label.

The well-known big brands of sparkling wine also rely on indifferent wines as a base. Popular though the big names may be, they owe their fame, and their inflated prices, not to excellence but to massive advertising campaigns. They are seldom good buys; at the bottom of the price scale there are much better buys around, sparklers without a famous name.

Most sparkling wines are available in a range of styles: sweet, medium, dry and pink. But Asti Spumante is only available sweet, and The Real Thing, only white. When dry drinks were first considered chic, Asti Spumante became a social casualty. But this was the wine snob's loss. Made from highly-scented muscat grapes, it is a pungent, though delicately fruity wine, and when it is young, fresh and chilled, quite excellent. Asti Spumante grapes come from a restricted area, and the price is slightly inflated as a consequence. Moscato Spumante has no such restrictions and is therefore priced very competitively. A pink version is available ... and pink sparkling wine is, after all, considered to be one of life's most frivolous luxuries.

 **MEALS FOR ONE**

MEALS FOR ONE

Jane Grigson's meal for one person is more than just a feast of ingenuity by one of Britain's leading scholar cooks. It's more, too, than a lesson in seasonal shopping or nutritional values (though it's those as well).

These recipes are the direct result of Jane's judging a *Food and Drink* challenge to produce a well-balanced meal for one person which cost under a pound and could be cooked on a single ring. The competitors were home economics students from four colleges of higher education.

When judging the entries, Jane expressed her disappointment with the lack of fresh food used. She felt that freshness and quality didn't have to be sacrificed to economy and nutrition, notwithstanding their importance. The winning team from Birmingham College of Food Technology came closest, in her opinion, to producing a tasty, fresh and appetising meal. At that point, Jane Grigson accepted the challenge and produced a meal of her own along the same lines. This had five distinct elements: three prepared courses, followed by cheese and fruit.

Carrot Salad

4 oz (100 gms) grated carrot
6 chopped green peppercorns
Black pepper
Thin slices of chilli
For the vinaigrette dressing:
$\frac{1}{2}$ tsp olive oil
$\frac{1}{4}$ tsp white wine vinegar
1 pinch French mustard
1 pinch salt

Make up the vinaigrette dressing by shaking all the ingredients together. Mix the carrot with the three different peppers and pour the dressing over.

Parsnip Soup

1 oz (25 gms) butter
1 chopped small onion
1 chopped clove garlic
1 peeled and diced parsnip
1 pinch curry powder
Water
Salt and pepper

Melt the butter in a pan, add the onion and garlic and cook over a medium heat until soft. Add the parsnip and toss with the onion. Add a small amount of curry powder, according to taste. Cook this for a further minute or two to release the flavour of the spices and then add enough water to cover the vegetables. Season with salt and pepper and simmer until the parsnip is soft, about 20 minutes.

Purée the soup in a blender or food processor. Serve with chopped parsley and a slice of wholemeal bread.

Devilled Sprats

6 or 7 sprats
Salt and cayenne pepper
1 tsp butter
1 wedge of lemon or lemon juice

Wash the sprats, although there is no need to gut them. Sprinkle lightly with salt and cayenne pepper to give a slightly devilled flavour. Lightly butter a non-stick frying pan and cook the sprats for approximately 4 minutes in their own natural oils, turning once or twice during cooking. Serve with lemon.

The three recipes given above can be made for under a pound and will still leave enough money to finish the meal with some cheese and fruit. Here is Jane Grigson's breakdown of the cost:

1 carrot	4p
1 parsnip	6p
Parsley	5p
6 oz (175 gms) sprats	16p
2 oz (50 gms) mature English farmhouse cheddar cheese	24p
1 Sharon fruit	28p
Total	83p

The remaining 17p would cover the cost of ingredients that Jane Grigson would normally have in the store cupboard, such as garlic and curry powder.

The winning recipes came from the Birmingham College of Food Technology and won because of their flavour, good nutritional content, freshness and appetising looks. The following two recipes can be made for a total cost of only 49p!

Cheesy Leek and Macaroni

1 oz (25 gms) margarine
1 oz (25 gms) brown breadcrumbs
3 oz (75 gms) leeks, cleaned, trimmed and roughly chopped
$\frac{1}{2}$ oz (10 gms) flour
$\frac{1}{4}$ pint (150 ml) milk
1 oz (25 gms) macaroni
2 oz (50 gms) cheddar cheese with onions and chives, grated
Salt and pepper
1 tbsp chopped fresh parsley

Melt half the margarine in a saucepan and fry the breadcrumbs for 1 minute. Keep the breadcrumbs on one side. Melt the rest of the margarine in the pan and sauté the leeks for about 2 minutes. Stir in the flour and cook gently for 1 minute, stirring all the while. Gradually stir in the milk to make a sauce. Bring to the boil and add the macaroni. Simmer for 5 minutes, stirring occasionally. Remove the pan from the heat and add the cheese. Season to taste. Pour into a serving dish and arrange the breadcrumbs and parsley, lattice-style, on the top. Serve hot.

Florida Salad

1 orange
$\frac{1}{2}$ grapefruit

Peel and slice the orange and grapefruit. Arrange attractively in a glass serving dish.

THE
FOOD & DRINK
£10 CHALLENGE

THE FOOD AND DRINK £10 CHALLENGE

Imagine that you're supervising the cooking of a ten-course banquet for 100 distinguished guests at one of London's leading hotels. Among the diners are six of Europe's greatest chefs. Since your budget is virtually unlimited, you've decided to have white truffles specially flown in from Italy at £300 a pound. With twenty minutes to go before the kick-off, the exotic fungi still haven't materialised. Question: what do you do? Answer: rapidly disguise yourself and emigrate.

However, Anton Mosimann, *Maître Chef des Cuisines* at the Dorchester, is made of sterner stuff. The nightmarish predicament I've described is exactly the one I found him in when we first met. The occasion was the launching of *The Official Foodie Handbook* in the hotel's Terrace Room. Happily for his gourmet friends and clients, Mosimann didn't take the first plane out of Heathrow. Instead he smiled stoically ... and so did Fate: moments later the delicacies arrived in perfect condition.

Great chefs aren't supposed to behave like that; the popular stereotype is of mountainous men, constantly at boiling point. Perhaps Mosimann owes his even temperament to his birthplace, Switzerland, and to the fact that he's been cooking ever since he was first tall enough to reach the pans. His parents ran a restaurant and farm so he learned from the grassroots, literally, about butchering and the preparation of fresh produce. After his Swiss training, he broadened his culinary education in Italy, Canada, Japan and France.

None of this can have fully prepared the *maître* for the great *Food and Drink* challenge. Impressed by his unflappability on the night of the missing truffles, we decided to put him to an even more demanding test. We would ask him to cook Sunday lunch for an ordinary family on their total budget of £10 – that wouldn't leave much change for flying in goodies from Italy. On BBC Local Radio in Sheffield we appealed for volunteers. Of the thirty families who replied, we chose the Wilcocks: John drives a council gully wagon, cleaning roadside drains, and Margaret works in a plastics factory. Joining them round their table would be their daughter, son-in-law and three grandchildren, seven in all. Mosimann, who's used to overseeing eighty well-equipped chefs at the Dorchester, would be working alone with the Wilcocks' utensils in a tiny council-house kitchen. Armed only with a box of knives, the man who's been called 'the greatest chef now cooking in England' set out for Sheffield, not knowing what to expect and keeping an open mind about the menu.

For their part, the Wilcocks were also slightly apprehensive. But their Saturday morning shopping trip with Mosimann in Sheffield market soon put them at ease. 'He was grand,' said John, 'he knew exactly what he wanted.' And he knew exactly how much he was prepared to pay for it. The *maître* bought two chickens (cheap at 38p a pound), and an appetising selection of fresh vegetables. His expression of injury and disdain when an unsuspecting stallholder offered him frozen Chinese rabbit was a masterpiece of mime.

Sunday morning at the Wilcocks was one they'll never forget. The box of knives came into its own as Mosimann deftly carved every last ounce of flesh from the chickens and chopped up the carcasses for stock. But the climax of the session was the emergence from the oven of the bread and butter pudding. The Wilcocks' version of the dish, as they frankly admitted, was a pretty stodgy affair which, when cold, might have served to plug a gap in the Great Wall of China. Here, though, was a confection as light as a soufflé. Consisting largely of buttered bread, eggs and double cream, it sat a little guiltily alongside Mosimann's theory of fatless *cuisine naturelle*, but the indulgence was still worth any future restorative – even the London Marathon.

The chicken fricassee, two vegetable dishes, the pudding and a bottle of red wine came to £9.88. For a few pence inside the limit, the *maître* had fed seven people superbly – and there were even some leftovers for later.

In the course of the exercise, both the Wilcocks and the *Food and Drink* viewers in general, had learned a number of important lessons: always buy fresh produce; look for the best price; and never, never overcook. To assess the effect of the experiment on John Wilcock's cooking, we went back to Sheffield a few months later for a BBC 2 *Food and Drink* Special. This time John would do the cooking, while Anton Mosimann sampled the results with the rest of the family. It could have been a bit like asking Ian Botham to umpire a game of beach cricket. But undaunted by the presence of his discerning guest, John chose a *carbonade de boeuf*, with Yorkshire pudding and mashed cauliflower, followed by Mosimann's own recipe for the famous bread and butter pudding.

The *maître* pronounced the *carbonade* tasty but gently suggested that if it had been cooked for an hour less it would have been even better. The Yorkshire pudding, the first he'd eaten that had been prepared by a Yorkshireman, was given full marks. And for the dessert, he could scarcely find praise enough. The earlier master-class had obviously paid off. John Wilcock had gained the confidence to be more adventurous and now regularly tries out his expanding repertoire on his friends.

The Sheffield story wasn't a gimmick. It was very much in line with the *Food and Drink* philosophy. Some restaurateurs would have you think differently, but we believe that there's no mystery about good, sensible eating. We can't all afford white truffles from Italy (and might not want them if we could), but we *can* be aware of quality and cost when we buy. We *can* prepare food thoroughly, and we *can* be aware that overcooking is the enemy of flavour. Above all, we *can* take a great chefs word for it that simple, fresh food is best. I'm sure our own crafty cook, Michael Barry, would agree wholeheartedly.

Now, here are the recipes with which Anton Mosimann entertained the Wilcock family.

Chicken Fricassee
(Serves four)

---

1 chicken
2 oz (50 gms) butter
Salt and freshly-ground pepper
1 chopped clove garlic
4 oz (100 gms) button onions
12 oz (350 gms) mixed peppers, red, green and yellow
4 oz (100 gms) button mushrooms
7 fl oz (200 ml) dry white wine
1 pint (600 ml) brown chicken stock
Fresh rosemary, thyme, marjoram and basil
8 oz (225 gms) diced tomatoes
Parsley, for decoration

The chicken should be drawn and singed and cut into eight pieces. (An oven-ready chicken can be used instead.) Melt the butter in a large pan, then season and sauté the chicken until light golden-brown. Remove the chicken and put to one side. Add a little garlic, the button onions and peppers to the pan and cook for a few minutes, then add the mushrooms, white wine and chicken stock and cook for a few more minutes.

Add the freshly-chopped herbs and tomatoes and replace the chicken. Cover and cook over a medium heat for about 10 to 15 minutes. Remove the chicken pieces and vegetables and keep hot. Reduce the sauce to the required consistency by boiling and adjust the seasoning to taste.

Arrange the chicken pieces and vegetables on a serving dish. Pour the sauce over and serve sprinkled with parsley.

Note: To ensure that this dish has a good colour, it is important not to over-cook the peppers.

Anton's Potato Pie
(Serves four to six)

This is a simple dish and, for the cholesterol-minded, it has the bonus of being fatless.

1½ lbs (700 gms) peeled potatoes
1 large onion
Salt and pepper
Pinch ground nutmeg
A little vegetable or chicken stock

Thinly slice the potatoes and onion. Toss them over heat in a non-stick pan then transfer them to an ovenproof dish. Season, sprinkle with the nutmeg and then moisten with a little vegetable or chicken stock. Cover and cook at gas mark 6, (400°F (200°C) for 30 minutes or until tender. Remove the cover for the final 10 minutes of cooking to allow the potatoes to brown.

Cabbage with Bacon
(Serves four to five)

This is Anton Mosimann's nifty way of transforming plain British cabbage. He uses savoy but any type of cabbage is suitable.

4 oz (100 gms) chopped unsmoked bacon
1 shredded cabbage
Salt and pepper
A little vegetable or chicken stock

Fry the bacon pieces in a non-stick pan. When they are crisp and golden, add the cabbage, seasoning and a little stock. Cover and boil for 2 to 3 minutes before serving.

Bread and Butter Pudding
(Serves four)

9 fl oz (250 ml) milk
9 fl oz (250 ml) double cream
Pinch salt
1 vanilla pod
3 eggs
5 oz (150 gms) sugar
3 small bread rolls, thinly sliced and buttered
1 oz (25 gms) butter
3 oz (75gms) sultanas, soaked in water overnight
1 tbsp apricot jam
A little icing sugar

Bring the milk, cream, salt and the vanilla pod to a gentle simmer. In a separate bowl, beat together the eggs and sugar. Stir in the hot milk and cream, removing the vanilla pod. Sieve the mixture. Arrange the bread in a greased ovenproof dish and add the sultanas. Pour in the liquid mixture and dot the remaining butter on top. Poach in a low oven, gas mark 2, 300°F (150°C) for 35 to 40 minutes in a bain-marie or a tray lined with newspaper and half-filled with water. When golden-brown on top, dot with apricot jam and dust with icing sugar. This is good served with double cream or bottled fruit.